Turning Losing Forex Trades into Winners

Founded in 1807, John Wiley & Sons is the oldest independent publishing company in the United States. With offices in North America, Europe, Australia and Asia, Wiley is globally committed to developing and marketing print and electronic products and services for our customers' professional and personal knowledge and understanding.

The Wiley Trading series features books by traders who have survived the market's ever-changing temperament and have prospered—some by reinventing systems, others by getting back to basics. Whether a novice trader, professional, or somewhere in-between, these books will provide the advice and strategies needed to prosper today and well into the future.

For a list of available titles, please visit our Web site at www.Wiley Finance.com.

Turning Losing Forex Trades into Winners

Proven Techniques to Reverse Your Losses

GERALD E. GREENE

WILEY

John Wiley & Sons, Inc.

Published by John Wiley & Sons, Inc., Hoboken, New Jersey
Published simultaneously in Canada

For general information on our other products and services or for technical support, please contact our Customer Care Department within the United States at (800) 762-2974, outside the United States at (317) 572-3993 or fax (317) 572-4002.

Wiley also publishes its books in a variety of electronic formats. Some content that appears in print may not be available in electronic books. For more information about Wiley products, visit our web site at www.wiley.com.

Library of Congress Cataloging-in-Publication Data:

Greene, Gerald E.
  Turning losing FOREX trades into winners : proven techniques to reverse your losses / Gerald E. Greene.
      p. cm. – (Wiley trading series)
  Includes bibliographical references and index.
  ISBN 978-0-470-18769-2 (cloth : alk. paper)
  1. Foreign exchange market.   2. Foreign exchange futures.   I. Title.
  HG3853.G737 2008
  332.4'5–dc22   2008012221

Printed in the United States of America

10 9 8 7 6 5 4 3 2 1

To my most patient and understanding wife Sharon, who supports my passion for helping Forex Traders.

To all Forex traders who have lost money to the brokers and banks. Hopefully this manuscript will help each and every reader succeed.

Contents

Foreword

If you use technical analysis, you are likely—or will be likely—to use candle charts. This is because candles can be used in any time frame and in any market, and they allow traders to spot turns before potentially large moves.

As the one who revealed this charting method to the Western world, it is gratifying to see its popularity. However, with the candle charts' universal availability and widespread use, there comes a downside—most traders are using them incorrectly. That is the reason my firm has such a strong focus on education (www.candlecharts.com/free-education).

One of the most dangerous and common misuses of candles is trying to use them as a stand-alone trading vehicle. This is wrong. Candles are a tool, not a trading system. This is why I also show how to combine candles with Western technical tools and to always incorporate risk/reward analysis.

Equally important is money management—that is, proper trade size. For example, what is the proper trade size to enter a position? How do you scale into or out of a trade? How do you adjust trade size for your risk tolerance level? These are important questions, but they are beyond the scope of my expertise. That is why I am pleased to strongly recommend this excellent book.

Based on working with some of the top institutional traders, I can tell you that many of the most successful ones have had more losses than gains. How did they accomplish this? The answer is by the judicious use of stops and proper trade size. So if you are picking up this book, congratulations: You have taken the first steps in following in the footsteps of such successful traders.

There is a Japanese Samurai saying, *"He whose ranks are united in purpose will be victorious."* By merging the timing advantages of candles with the discipline of proven money management as revealed in *A Trader's Money Management System,* you will become a more confident and successful trader. As an extra bonus, you will have less stress!

Steve Nison, president of Candlecharts.com
Author of *Japanese Candlestick Charting Techniques*
www.candlecharts.com

Acknowledgments

I would like to pay tribute to my friend and colleague Donald Snellgrove, who has probably done more than any other person in the world to help Forex traders. Unfortunately the Forex market is so very difficult to work with that most traders who attempt it do not succeed without help.

As a member of the Concorde Forex Group mentoring team, I have been personally associated with more than a thousand Forex traders over the past five years, and I have appreciated their sincerity and eagerness to learn. Our working together has contributed to my success and to the development of this manuscript. I have seen many Forex traders fail and give up. I have seen many Forex traders jump from one trading system to another in an attempt to succeed. They have taught me many things for which I am grateful. But, their struggle for success is the main reason for writing this book in order to assist them and all other Forex traders who need to know how to manage the losing Forex trade.

Introduction

Most trading systems and methodologies that I have been exposed to are able to achieve 80 percent success at their best. In any market there is a reason for this as conditions change without prior notice. The market for any product or currency alternates between three stages that I will call trending, channeling, and transitioning. A market is trending when it is moving consistently in one direction. A market is channeling when it is bouncing between levels like a ping-pong ball. The periods between these two major stages is the transitioning market. It is difficult for the trader to be good in all of these conditions. Trading systems tend to do well when the market is trending, but then fail during the other two stages.

I remember talking to a trader during a Forex trade show who described how his professional money manager had built up his account over 60 percent the previous year. However, during the 90 days leading up to the trade show, he had many losing trades, and the account balance had returned to the previous level. I immediately knew what had happened. The U.S. dollar was trending during the previous year, and now it was not. This was the same trade show where two companies introduced their new automatic trading software, which is always exciting to contemplate. During discussions with the two firms, they admitted that the current quarter was not working very well, and that they were suffering losses. Again, the current quarter was not a trending one, and they were suffering as a result. These trading systems could not accommodate the different stages. The market makers are ruthless, and they are always looking for easy money—yours.

Remember the Seinfeld episode where George convinced Jerry to buy stock based upon an inside tip? Well, the stock went down and reached Jerry's 50 percent level, so he panicked and bailed out. You can guess the rest even if you did not see the episode. Sure enough, within a few days the stock went up reaching Jerry's 150 percent level, and he was distraught. I know that you are thinking that it reached the Fibonacci 50 percent level and then resumed its upward course. But, if you look at your charts carefully, you will find that these Fibonacci levels are close together, and if

1

you use the word "approximate" the reversal can take place at almost any level. Traders look back and identify the reversal point with authority, and wonder how they missed that wonderful technical indicator. If you trade the 50 percent levels every time they are reached, however, you will not be successful.

There are many trading advisors who have ideas regarding the selection process and how to pick the right times to trade retracements, but overall, it is difficult to exceed the 80 percent success rate.

Trading systems work with the obvious two choices:

1. When to enter the market in the same direction
2. When to enter the market in the opposite direction

So, if you are trading a system carefully or just anticipating with your gut, you will benefit from tactical knowledge for what I call "cost averaging." Average the results of one bad trade followed by one good trade. Leave behind the emotional baggage of a bad trade and then be ready to take advantage of the market cycles at the right moment to offset losses, either partially or completely.

Whether your trading system is based upon fundamental knowledge of economics or on charting technical analysis doesn't matter. You will occasionally find yourself with open trades that are not working, and at that point I can help you take advantage of market conditions to improve your position.

"How can I succeed when my trading will not be 100 percent right?" If you have this question in your mind, then this book is for you. I will describe a method for you to analyze difficult trading situations. I will not attempt to alter your trading style or trading system, but I will help you understand how to get out of a trade that is not working for you and how to recover from many losing situations.

CHAPTER 1

Trading Systems

The number of Forex trading systems available today is very large. The Internet contains descriptions of each one with promises of untold wealth awaiting the trader who uses it. An obvious question arises in our minds: "If each one works, then why did someone need to develop the next one?" During the past six years I have worked with hundreds of Forex traders who have struggled to find a method of trading that works for them. I am not a psychologist, but it seems to me that trading systems, or styles, need to match the personality type. It is amazing to observe this in action. There are people who can trade specific systems with ease, while others just cannot make it work for them. The same trader will move to a different trading system and suddenly succeed. Some traders keep looking, while others give up, but the persistent seeker usually finds a method that fits, which results in a positive trading experience. So, the beginning trader faces two challenges. The first is to identify a trading system that matches his/her personality, and the second is to master the system itself. Over the years, the people group that I have seen struggle the most with trading systems are male engineers. They have two issues to deal with. First, they are engineers because they like to find better ways of doing things. Their first self-appointed task is typically to find a way to improve any trading system that they are attempting to learn. Instead of following the system, and learning how to use it, they work on the system itself, and postpone for a later time learning how to trade it. And, of course, because they are males, they hesitate to ask for directions. Based upon what I just said, you can guess that women make good traders because they are willing to follow directions. Yes, I believe that to be true.

TRADER AUDIT

The simplest way to determine if the system is working for you is the net profit/loss statement. There is, however, another important measurement that every trader should make at least once a year, and that is what I call the "Trader Audit." The Trader Audit is a simple examination of losing trades. I recommend that you review your trade history for the last 12 months and list a sample of the losing trades. The sample size is subjective, but should contain at least a dozen losers. Write them on a sheet of paper, or use a computer spreadsheet, leaving space for five columns of information to the right of the trade. Record the currency pair, entry date and time, entry price, close date and time, close price, and pips per lot lost. When this is completed, add the headings for the new information to the right of the pips lost data. The five new headings are +10, +20, +30, +40 and +50. The purpose is to evaluate the Forex history and determine the outcome if the stop loss value for these losing trades had been larger. Quite often traders who are entering at the right time are also setting the stop loss incorrectly, and not giving the Forex market enough room to breathe. By reviewing the history, and filling in the new values of profit/loss with the larger stops, it is easy to recalculate the overall profit/loss. So, when the numbers are entered in each column, the next step is to calculate the total for each new column. If any of the right-most five columns renders a higher overall profit, then it is clear that larger stops would have been better. If none of the right-most five columns renders more profit, then the trades were "bad" entries to begin with.

This simple exercise helps the trader to identify the area that requires the most improvement. Either way, you can use this study to guide your efforts moving forward. You can readily understand why this audit should be performed on a regular basis. Not only do we sometimes get lazy, but the Forex behavior also changes from year to year. In Figure 1.1 the first entry was stopped out with a 25 pip loss. If the stop loss had been set 10 pips higher, the trade would have been successful. The second example is different, and shows that the stop needed to be 20 pips higher. I can conclude that if my stops on these two transactions were just 20 more pips than I used (see P20 column), it would have made a 92-pip difference per lot to the account balance. Using this technique, you will be able to determine if your stops are too tight.

CURRENCY	OPEN	ACTION	CLOSE	PRICE	LIMIT	STOP	LOSS	P10	P20	P30	P40	P50
EUR/USD	Mar 28 04:00	SELL	Mar 28 10:00	1.3337	1.3317	1.3362	-25	20	20	20	20	20
EUR/USD	Apr 08 08:30	BUY	Apr 08 12:30	1.3398	1.3415	1.3368	-30	-40	-50	17	17	17
TOTAL							-55	-20	-30	37	37	37

FIGURE 1.1   Trader Audit

BROKER CONSIDERATIONS

One of the things that each trader needs to understand is that the broker needs time to move money when it is traded. For example, if a trader enters a buy on the EUR/USD for 10 lots, and the market is moving and it goes up three pips within two minutes, and then the trader closes the trade, the broker can be caught with the money stuck in his system. That is, the broker might not have been able to pass the transaction through to a bank, and it is caught with the loss. Brokers do not like "scalpers," which is what I just described. They want traders who will remain in positions long enough for them to clear the transaction, especially if the trader is trading a "mini" account which uses non-standard size lots.

Mini account trades need to be accumulated by the broker until a standard lot size is reached, and then a transaction can be made with a bank. The broker computer software is becoming more sophisticated and is able to evaluate customer accounts to identify scalpers. If they determine that a customer is causing them to lose profit, then they will take action to prevent future losses. The landscape is changing, however, whereby the banks are developing computer systems that allow them to offer trading directly to the retail customers. But, the banks are just as sensitive to the issue of scalping. The Forex broker might be an endangered species as banks become more aggressive and offer retail services.

Some brokers have very lean operations that involve a small support staff and a computer server. For example, a broker can license the MetaTrader© (Copyright MetaQuotes Software Corp.) trading platform and outsource the server to a firm that specializes in this platform. It is a simple process, and requires little or no skills, and no software engineers. Standard software interfaces are used to connect to banks, and the broker is in business almost overnight. But, mini accounts need to be handled separately, so there is a software interface to allow for this. The broker can have its own dealing desk where partial lots are accumulated and traded with the banks, or the broker can use the software to give this business to another broker who has a dealing desk. You would be amazed at how much consolidation has developed, and how much business ultimately goes through very few dealing desks.

FUNDAMENTALS

The system of trading that relies on the fundamental economic factors is a sound one. There is no voodoo there. It makes sense, but it requires full knowledge of all of the factors, and it requires very fast analysis as daily announcements are made. It is amazing to watch the Forex in action when the various governments make an announcement. The larger banks have predefined tables of what they will do based upon the expected economic values to be reported. However, when the numbers released are unexpected, then large market swings occur. I know of one trader who trades a large number of lots with a Swiss bank, and who trades the fundamental announcements. He claims a success rate of over 90 percent. He says he has a fast finger, and enters his trades very quickly with very good results. I don't know about this. If you were the banker and at the end of the year evaluated his trading account and had your computer prepare a profit and loss statement that showed commissions gained, but also showed that every time you sold to this guy the bank lost potential profits within seconds, you would probably ask him to take his business elsewhere.

There is, of course, the basic way to trade fundamentals that entails a larger view. If you determine that the U.S. dollar will weaken over the next year, and enter a long-term trade accordingly, then this is a good thing. But most Forex traders are short-term traders, or what we will call Day-Traders. When trading with high leverage of 100 or 200 to 1, one needs to be very accurate.

TECHNICAL TRADING

My first entry into the stock market was a primitive form of technical trading. I was involved in the medical surgical instrument business, and we sold several patented products that we developed, plus others that were developed by physician partners. In the course of our business a competitor emerged with what I thought was a better product than one of ours. After we sold our business to a larger firm that was listed on the NYSE, I began to purchase this ex-competitor's stock. I would look at the daily chart on the Internet and place orders to buy whenever the stock price dipped. This would result in almost one transaction per day as I would buy the retracements and sell the recoveries. The stock price did not move that much, but the price was small and the percentage of movement was correspondingly large, and because it was a new and effective surgical product that was not subject to economic recessions, I knew that the overall trend was upward. I congratulated myself for doing so well.

After three months the stock prices moved differently so I stayed out of the market to wait for a better price, and one day the price jumped and nearly doubled. This was my first lesson in the weakness of technical trading. The fundamental trader would have been more patient.

My next trade was more fundamental. I found a female hormone therapy product that was made from natural products. It was designed to replace the standard one that was based upon horse mare urine. Now, I thought to myself, when women find out about this new product and the issues involved, there will be a large shift in market share. So, I purchased all I could afford and waited. The price went down initially, but then it tripled in price prior to the acquisition by a large pharmaceutical company, whereupon I liquidated my positions. Now, these two examples make fundamental trading look pretty good. It also gives the impression that technical trading is less advantageous. In fact, there are some who call technical trading "voodoo" trading.

If you parse a technical chart, you will notice that all of the retracement/recoveries far outweigh the straight line. Is it possible to trade all of these oscillations? Is there a safe way to enter and exit the market to get in on this action? This is the quest of the technical trader. Just give me a little bit of each oscillation, and I will do quite well, thank you.

The fundamentalist will always identify a reason that the market moved after the fact. This, to me, has always been suspect. Today, for example, the market responded lightly to a given change in economic conditions, while yesterday it did not, revealing this to be lacking in credibility for me.

The technical analyst will point to a compilation of evidence that supports the contention that the technical indicators are "prophetic." Quite often the technicals are telling the market how to respond to economic news. I have observed this enough to become convinced that it is possible for anyone to trade successfully with full reliance on the technical indicators. In fact, this is my preference at the present time.

It seems to me that the trader's choice of technical indicators is purely subjective and that, when used properly, they all tend to work. The key to success is to use them consistently, and to rely on more than one time compression for clarity.

In my opinion, it is not necessary to use more than two or three oscillators to trade. I remember talking to a trader at a trade show in Florida who had his laptop computer with him. He was very animated about how he traded so well using his charting, and as he was describing his charts I could not help but be amazed at how he could even see the candlesticks because there were so many oscillators. To me, it was crazy, but to him, it worked because he used them consistently.

ILLUSTRATIONS

Have you ever noticed that illustrations in books and magazines for investment trading always seem to select the best trading conditions? When illustrating an Elliott Wave, the example always has perfectly defined

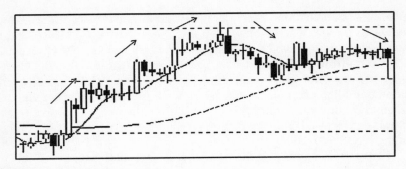

FIGURE 1.2   Elliot Wave
Source: Copyright © 2007, Concorde Forex Group, Inc.

movement that gives the trader a perfect opportunity to take advantage of every other trader in the market. Figures 1.2 and 1.3 are the best examples that I could find. Actually, examples of perfect trades are few and far between. The trader is usually in a gray area, not knowing for sure what to do.

When showing an example of channel boundaries, the market bounces off the exact value where the trendline is drawn. Oh, wouldn't that be nice!

Figures 1.2 and 1.3 make the point, but the market behaves like this only on rare occasions. We are shown by someone a perfect template, and then we are on our own to identify the correct times to declare to ourselves when a match occurs.

In this book, I have carefully selected illustrations to help you understand the market when the conditions are not fully clear. These gray areas are quite often difficult to understand, so I have created a notebook of actual market examples for myself to reference when trading. This helps me

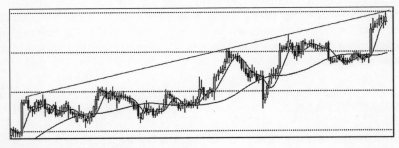

FIGURE 1.3   Trendwall Bounce
Source: Copyright © 2007, Concorde Forex Group, Inc.

more fully understand the gray market conditions and how to avoid the bad entries.

It is very helpful for the technical trader to identify specific trades and to give them labels. The River X, Trendwall Breakout, Trendwall Breakin, RiverBend, and Fibanocci Bounce are examples. Once labels are applied, then the technical criteria can be defined, documented, and illustrated. When this is completed the trader can gain expertise in searching for, and trading, these patterns.

Trend

The most important factor in technical trading is the "Trend." The trend is the trader's assessment of the overall market direction. This is a very subjective assessment because it is used to support the trading style of the trader. For example, if the weekly trend is up then the long-term trader will be trading in that direction, but if the five-minute trend is down, the short-term trader will be trading down. Once again, I am suggesting that the trader fully categorize the trading style so these supporting decisions will be fully applicable and relevant at all times. When using eight time compressions, two moving average lines, and one oscillator, there are nearly 200 factors to consider when deciding what the trend is. This is nearly overwhelming to the trader. But, this factor is so very important that it cannot be ignored.

Let me ask then, "Have you clearly defined the criteria for identifying the trend each time you enter a trade?" This is a critical issue, and I believe that you cannot succeed without a correct trend assessment.

We have all been told the "day" chart is the "truth" chart. I have wondered where in the day chart is the truth? Is it the color of the current candlestick? Is it the slow-moving average line? How about the fast-moving average line? Or, is it the oscillators that I am using at the bottom of my chart? You can easily understand how confusing this can be. But, you must come to a clear understanding for yourself and for your trading style.

Day traders, it seems to me, who enter and exit the market in a matter of minutes or hours, should be careful to use a trend that is relevant to their trading, and not be overly influenced by what professional traders say. So, if you are trading short-term trades, then your trend must be based upon short-term factors. The "truth" chart for you might be the four-hour, or even the two-hour, chart. Now that you have narrowed the scope of truth to a selected time compression, you next need to decide what technical indicators best reflect the trend over time. This might require you to perform a detailed study to make that determination. For day trading, I prefer to use the two-hour chart. Inside the two-hour chart, I prefer to use an oscillator. When the candles are going up, and the oscillator fast line is above the slow line and is going up, then for me, the trend is up. This oscillator could be Slow Stochastic, MACD, or any other one that you desire. But, for me, this is a reliable way to determine the short-term trend.

Notice in Figure 1.4, which includes a Stochastic oscillator, how fairly consistent the market is defined as the oscillations are made on this two-hour chart.

The example of Figure 1.4 is fairly consistent, but sometimes you will find the oscillator going one way while the market goes the other. This is called "divergence," and will be more fully described later in Chapter 2. The next example, depicted in Figure 1.5, shows the MACD as it reveals the trend.

The trader needs to be careful to not allow the trends for other terms to confuse the issues. For example, a short-term trend might be up, while a medium-term trend might be down. When trading, one must keep very narrowly focused on the trend that supports the trade. Otherwise, you will become confused and lose confidence in the technical indicators.

This book is predicated upon the assessment of the trend and a clear judgment prior to entering any trade. You see, there is a great amount of

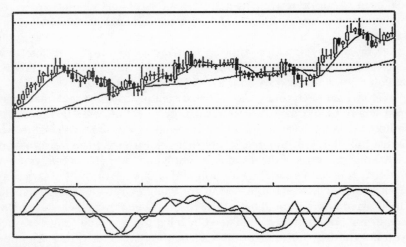

FIGURE 1.4 Oscillations
Source: Copyright © 2007, Concorde Forex Group, Inc.

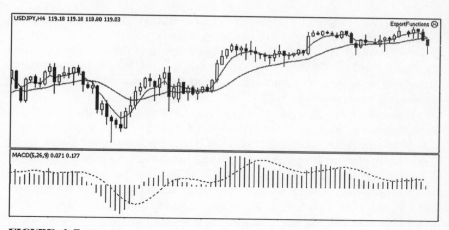

FIGURE 1.5 MACD
Source: Copyright 2001–2007, MetaQuotes Software Corp.

safety when trading with the trend. If you are trading with the trend and something goes wrong, then there is an opportunity to make multiple entries to support the initial entry. If you are trading with the trend, the only concern is if the trend changes in the middle of a trade. There will be an extensive discussion of trends in Chapter 2.

MARKET ANATOMY

Every trading system that I have seen uses either a moving average oscillator or some oscillating indicator. Decisions are made by the trader when the fast line crosses the slow line. In theory this is elegant and works every time. But, in practice the banks make the Forex market move sufficiently to make sure that no oscillator will work more than 80 percent of the time. The example given shows a chart with a basic slow- and fast-moving average. If you were to enter a trade up every time the fast line crossed the slow line going up, then you would observe that the best performance that you could achieve is 20 percent of trades where there were immediate profits. My studies have shown that 80 percent of these types of trades have retracements before they render profit. "Well then," you ask, "why not just wait for the retracement?" That is a good question, and if you are willing to let the other 20 percent go by, then it would be a good thing to do. The other 20 percent of trades look so good, and develop so cleanly, that you will be disappointed to watch them go by without you. The key here is for the trader to understand the anatomy of the market. The Elliot

Wave is a good example to start with. The market surges upward three times with two retracements followed by a larger reversal. Unfortunately, this does not always work, but the trader is looking for an edge — an indication of what the market is about to do. If two cycles have developed, then how often does the third also develop? I believe that this is a valid tactical decision process.

Figure 1.6 shows an example of what is referred to as a river X, where the two moving average lines cross each other. In the example you will notice that to the right of the X there is a pull-back or retracement (indicated where the moving average fast line dips down) followed by a surge in the market. This is one of those market behaviors that is repeatable and dependable. Many trading systems rely upon this behavior, and have developed a sound methodology of stops and limits to make consistent profits. But, the key here is to easily recognize and understand the anatomy. There are occasional anatomical malformations that the trader needs to be aware of, and the trader might often choose to not trade under these conditions. So, if the retracement is so severe that it forms a new river going the other way, the trader needs to assess the market and determine if it is safe to trade under those conditions. One must always maintain the attitude of a "shopper" seeking the best bargains, and always be willing to wait for a better opportunity.

Once the trader is fully skilled in the subject of market anatomy, then the next step of technical indicator interpretation can be more easily learned.

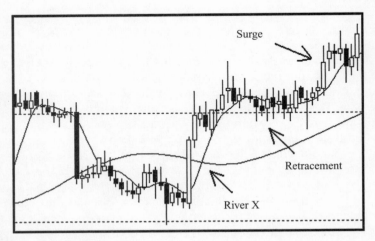

FIGURE 1.6 Market Anatomy
Source: Copyright © 2007, Concorde Forex Group, Inc.

TECHNICAL INDICATORS

The number of indicators available to the trader is probably infinite. Each trader examines them and narrows them down to a comfort level. But, let's face it; an indicator can only examine historical data, and virtually every trend has an end. Their effectiveness, therefore, is limited and sometimes very misleading. There are several categories of indicators from which to choose.

- Average Based
- Fibonacci Based
- Trend Based
- ABCD - Parallelogram
- Divergence Based

Average-Based Indicators

The average-based indicators are used heavily by most traders. The number of data points averaged depends upon the style of trading, but it all boils down to the same thing: When the average changes a little, the trader expects the average to change more. The challenge, of course, is that this is a trailing indicator. It does not anticipate. It only reports historical moves, whether it is three or fifty data points. Because this is a trailing indicator, it must be used with caution and cannot be relied upon as the major indicator. I can show you as many examples where an oscillator that reports averages fails as much as it succeeds. Its best use, therefore, is in conjunction with other charting tools that I will explain later.

Let me cite one example of how I use this indicator. Each day at noon Eastern time in the United States the London traders end their day, and the market tends to slow down. Quite often the market will even begin a retracement. When this happens, it becomes apparent on the 60-minute chart, as the fast-moving average line begins to change direction, and the other oscillators also cross and change direction. In the next example notice how the fast-moving average line has just begun to change direction where the vertical line is drawn, while the oscillator below has already changed direction. Waiting for the moving average to change direction is just a precaution, and gives me two reasons to enter this trade downward. This reversal might occur anytime between noon and midnight, but I prefer the ones that develop after 6:00 p.m. Eastern time. This trade is usually good for between ten and twenty pips per lot. I want this pattern to emerge as a lazy turn like the one shown in Figure 1.7. If the market overshoots, returns, and then tries a lazy turn, it is not as reliable because the stop loss

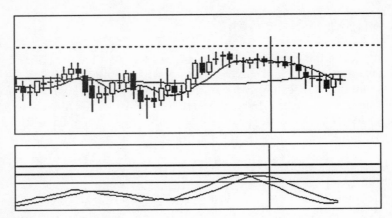

FIGURE 1.7 Sleeper Trade
Source: Copyright © 2007, Concorde Forex Group, Inc.

value is too high. One of the nice things about this trade is the very small stop loss value, which is about ten pips above the highest value to the left before the reversal began. I call this my "sleeper trade" because it develops while I sleep.

Fibonacci-Based Indicators

The Fibonacci-based indicators are one of the indicators that truly antic-ipate future movement. Most experienced traders like this one because it attempts to interpret the other traders' intentions. Markets are over-bought and oversold due to human illogical and emotive trading. Market surges are always followed by retracements. We, as a people, are pre-dictable to certain degrees. If we are anticipating a retracement, and are looking for it, we might be able to take advantage of it when it begins to show itself. Then the challenge is to determine the extent to which it will retrace. Once again, I make use of the one-hour chart, and its moving average to set up the scenario for the Fibonacci tool. When the moving average fast line changes direction, I am able to evaluate the entire range of the previous move and calculate the various Fibonacci levels. In the ex-ample shown in Figure 1.8, the top and bottom of the range are marked. Notice that the bottom and top are determined where the moving average fast line changed direction. I then have used the most extreme wick posi-tion in that range for the calculation. Five horizontal lines have been drawn, showing the bottom, top, .50, .382 and .618 Fibonacci levels. Incidentally, my own trading rules stipulate that if, during this retracement, either the moving average fast line changes direction again, or if the oscillator at the

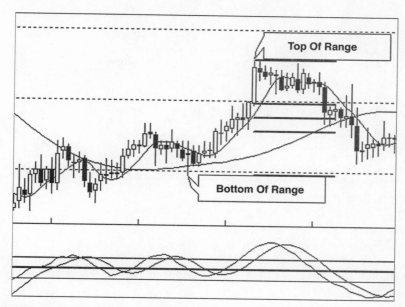

FIGURE 1.8 Fibonacci Indicator
Source: Copyright © 2007, Concorde Forex Group, Inc.

bottom crosses up, or my stop loss level is reached, I will exit the trade and not wait for the Fibonacci levels to be reached.

Most traders use the Fibonacci tool in conjunction with other tools and do not rely upon it as a stand-alone decision maker.

Trend-Based Indicators

There are two different, but similar, ways to measure the trend. The first is a simple straight line connecting various resistance or support points as shown in Figure 1.9

The second way to measure a trend is with a "Heart Line Based Trend Wall," which is much different than the simple trend line shown in Figure 1.9. The heart line is first calculated as an average for all the data in the range. This is a simple straight line right through the middle of the data. The next step is to create parallel lines to the heart line and push them outward. One line is pushed up, and one line is pushed down. Each line is pushed outward until there are just two wicks touching it. See the example of Figure 1.10.

In Figure 1.10, I show both types of lines to illustrate the superiority of the Trend Walls over the Trend Lines. Notice the breakout of the Trend

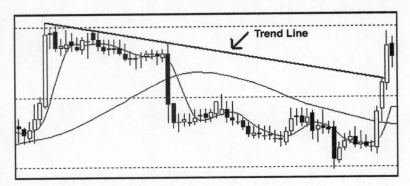

FIGURE 1.9   Trend Line
Source: Copyright © 2007, Concorde Forex Group, Inc.

Walls occurs much earlier than the breakout of the Trend Line, which gives
the trader who uses them a distinct advantage. There are specific rules
for trading the Trend Wall breakouts, and they can be learned from repu-
table training firms.

ABCD - Parallelogram Indicators

This indicator is closely related to the Fibonacci concept because it is
projecting future behavior based upon past behavior. It presumes that
every surge following a retracement will be the same height as the surge

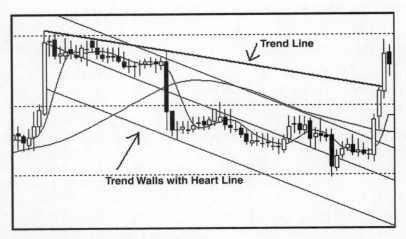

FIGURE 1.10   Trend Lines & Trend Walls
Source: Copyright © 2007, Concorde Forex Group, Inc.

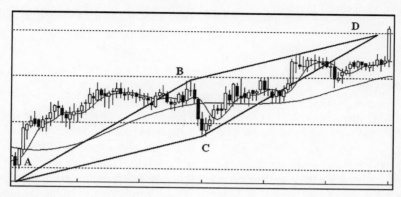

FIGURE 1.11 A-B-C-D
Source: Copyright © 2007, Concorde Forex Group, Inc.

that occurred before the retracement. This is pretty simple as shown in Figure 1.11 (Notice the A-B-C-D designations). This does not always work, so the trader needs to be cautious and use this along with other charting tools to find multiple reasons for any trading decision.

Divergence Indicators

Divergence is a common occurrence that presents itself to the technical trader when the market goes one way, while at the same time the oscillator goes the other as shown in Figure 1.12. Because oscillators are actually

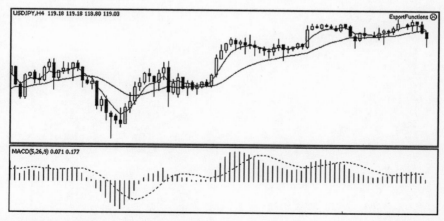

FIGURE 1.12 MACD Divergence
Source: Copyright 2001–2007, MetaQuotes Software Corp.

trailing indicators, they can mislead. I will talk more about this issue in Chapter 3.

SUMMARY

Trading indicators have limited reliability, and are typically used comparatively. The technical trader looks for multiple reasons to enter the market at a given point. Some traders wait until they find up to five different reasons to enter the market before entering the trade. This takes advantage of those moments where multiple trading systems are reaching the same conclusion to enter the market at the same time, which in and of itself causes the market to move as desired by the trader.

CHAPTER 2

Trend Lines & Trend Walls

The "trend" is such an important component of technical trading that I want to spend time to help you more fully understand its application. As I said in the previous chapter, there are two kinds of trends—the simple "Trend Line" and the more complex "Trend Wall," which is based upon a "Heart Line."

EXAMPLES OF TREND LINES

Many traders attempt to use the Trend Line breakout approach to trading. Whenever the market opens outside the line, then the trader will enter a trade in that direction. See the example in Figure 2.1 where the trader would enter down. In this example I have drawn the trend line at the approximate angle of the five-minute-moving average line. This is an arbitrary decision. Some traders prefer to wait for a support level to be established before drawing the trend line.

In Figure 2.2 is an example where a retracement has created a support point before the trend line is drawn.

Both of these examples are wonderful market entries where everything works right. But, this is not the normal behavior. Take a look Figure 2.3, which is quite typical. The line is drawn along the fast-moving average line. The first breakout candle opens outside the line, and the trader would enter down at that point. But, the market immediately moves up, which places the trader in a losing position. To add insult to injury, the market then

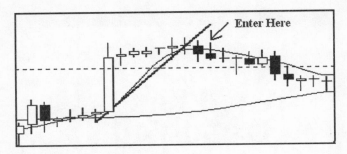

FIGURE 2.1 Trend Line Breakout
Source: Copyright © 2007, Concorde Forex Group, Inc.

moves rapidly upward while the trader is waiting for the next breakout, or worse yet, is still in the first trade hoping that it will return. The market does return inside the old line, which for some traders is a signal to enter going up. But, notice that the market immediately breaks out again. If a trader is trading these breakouts, then another bad trade would be made at this point. Another challenge for these trades is how to calculate the stop-loss value.

The best way to trade using these lines is to be a "shopper" and enter only when you can legitimately use a very small stop value. If you entered the first breakout in Figure 2.3, the stop-loss value would have needed to be very high. So, it is not a good candidate. The second breakout stop-loss value would be near the top of the previous candle, which looks acceptable to me. The ratio of stop loss and limit comes into play, and on this type of trade the limits are typically substantial, and if it is a good trade, then the market will not retrace (see breakout in Figure 2.2). The examples shown

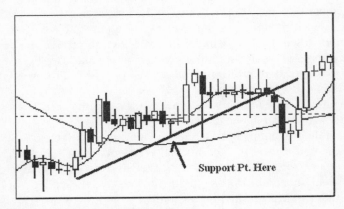

FIGURE 2.2 Trend Line Support Points
Source: Copyright © 2007, Concorde Forex Group, Inc.

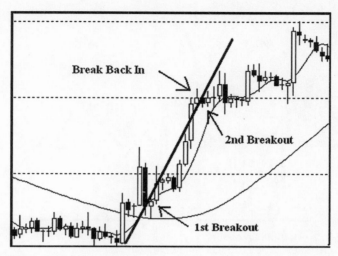

FIGURE 2.3 Trend Line Breakouts
Source: Copyright © 2007, Concorde Forex Group, Inc.

here are from a 4-hour chart, which gives the trader substantial pips per candle. So, the way to trade with trend lines is to be a shopper and then to be a strict disciplinarian. Accept the good trades only, and don't mess around with trades that are indecisive.

If we use the same example above, and draw a second trend line after the retracement, we see similar results (see Figure 2.4). The first

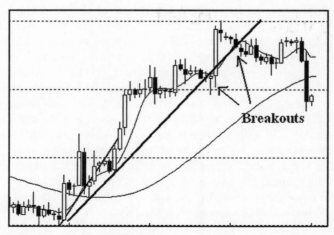

FIGURE 2.4 Trend Line Breakouts
Source: Copyright © 2007, Concorde Forex Group, Inc.

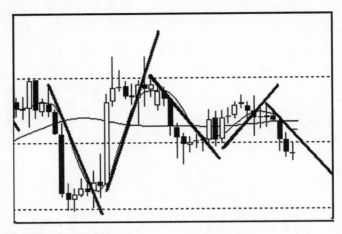

FIGURE 2.5 Multiple Breakouts
Source: Copyright © 2007, Concorde Forex Group, Inc.

breakout does not work, and the second is not very good either. It even has a break-in, which would be a very bad trade.

Figure 2.5 is a trader's dream. Notice how well these breakouts worked. The first one was the best, while the second one would have been stopped out for a loss, unless a trailing stop was used. I generally will move my stop to guarantee profit when there are 15 or more pips profit showing on the dealing station. The third and fourth would have been moderately successful. Ironically enough, this type of thrashing market in a tight channel with so many reversals is typically a severe challenge for most trading systems that rely upon a clear trend.

Trading with a "Heart Line"-based trend wall is much different, with similar but different objectives. This type of trading tool is used to trade market bounces off the inside of the walls and also the breakouts. Next is an example of a bounce; in fact, there are several bounces. These trend walls were created with the use of the first 14 candles only. You can see the old trend walls moving downward in the lower left of the example. The breakout is clear, but it is followed by a modest retracement. After the market recovered, the trend walls are drawn to make an estimate of where the market might go. The first thought that goes through the trader's mind is to take advantage of every bounce off the bottom wall, and you can see several in this example. The challenge is to pick the right ones, and to not pick the last one that does *not* bounce. Notice in this example that it is actually safer to trade the bounces off the top wall, which is trading against the trend. Let me show you some entries on the next example in Figure 2.6.

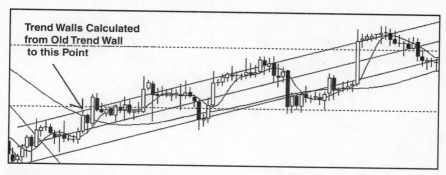

FIGURE 2.6 Heart Line-Based Trend Wall
Source: Copyright © 2007, Concorde Forex Group, Inc.

Here are 10 entry points as the market bounces off the top wall while going up. If the trader was patient and looking for small moves, then there were many opportunities for profit using this technique. There are times, although fairly rare, when the market will blow through the upper wall and never come back, but the majority of the time bounces will develop off these walls.

I would like to stress, once again, that because you know that a very high percentage of the time the market will return and pay profits, you can presume the bounce will occur; the other wall does not have the same success rate, because the final breakout is always in that direction.

Later in this chapter I will describe how to set the stop-loss value for these trades.

EXAMPLES OF TREND WALLS

Trading the top wall bounces is actually trading against the trend, which requires careful entry (see Figure 2.7). Trading the bottom wall has a built-in danger because the last bounce turns into a breakout when the trend ends. So, there is a trade-off regarding the advantages of each type of entry. A trader who understands how to use trend walls can easily trade the bounces off either wall. The detail entry description is shown in a later example.

A good practice is to scroll the charts back into history and draw these trend walls and paper trade, or practice without actually trading. It is best to constantly recalculate these walls as new candles develop. Leaving some old walls can also be beneficial as the old walls are quite often honored by the market. Sometimes inner walls develop that can be traded also.

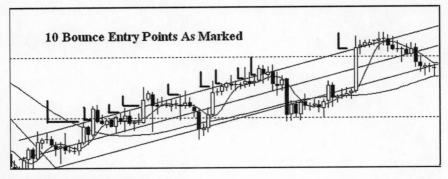

FIGURE 2.7 Trend Wall Bounce
Source: Copyright © 2007, Concorde Forex Group, Inc.

Let me show you some additional examples. Figure 2.8 shows an inner trend wall, which is actually the old trend wall created when this breakout was just a few candles old. Let me point out that I wait until the fast-moving average line changes direction once before attempting to predict the new trend. In this case, the inner trend wall shows the old channel. You can easily locate the entry points for trades up as the market bounces off the bottom trend wall. Later I will describe in detail how to recover losses to a large extent on breakouts after you have entered a bounce trade against the trend. Yes, this bounce trade is against the trend, at least on this particular

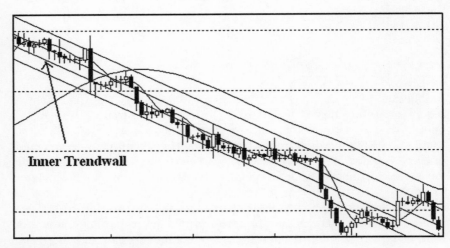

FIGURE 2.8 Inner Trend Wall
Source: Copyright © 2007, Concorde Forex Group, Inc.

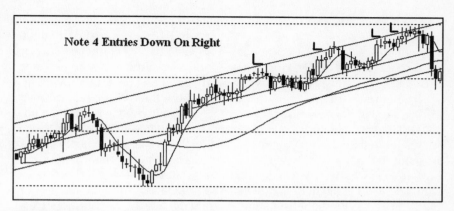

FIGURE 2.9 Trend Wall Bounces
Source: Copyright © 2007, Concorde Forex Group, Inc.

time compression. If the day chart and the month chart trend indicators are both going up, and the four-hour chart indicators are going down, then it is understandable that this type of trade could be very effective.

Figure 2.9 shows a large breakout downward, followed by a break back inside and then four separate bounces (marked with L's) off the upper trend wall before the final breakout down.

There is another phenomenon that is noteworthy: the propensity of the first candle breakout on the downside to continue in that direction. The 25th candle to the right of the leftmost candle is a small dark one just below the bottom trend wall. This is generally indicative of the market deciding to move in that direction on a larger scale. The second phenomenon is a similar one regarding the break-in candle. Notice to the right that, once back inside the trend walls, the candles tend to move upward.

DRILL-DOWN ENTRY

Once you have identified an opportunity where the market is approaching a trend wall on a larger time compression, it is risky to immediately enter the market. It is better to look for another reason to enter the market in the same direction using a smaller time compression. I prefer to draw the trend walls on the four-hour time compression. When the market approaches a trend wall on that compression, I then look at the 10-minute time compression and wait for the oscillator at the bottom of the chart to cross in the direction of my trade. This is a very important step, because if the market does not bounce where I expect it to, but continues to move through the trend wall, then the 10-minute oscillator typically does not cross back until the breakout is finished. In any event, when I enter from the 10-minute time compression, I also set the stop-loss value based on the last support point to the left of the entry candlestick on that same time compression. This limits my exposure for losses, while maintaining my target for profit.

In Figure 2.10 I am going to show you how this "drill-down" process works. We will begin with a picture of a four-hour chart with trend walls. To the left you will notice the old trend walls going down. We will begin our example with the first candle following the breakout to the upside. At the point of the breakout the new trend walls have not been drawn, and we have no idea where they will develop. But, we do know that the new trend is up, and we will begin to find reasons to trade in that direction.

Figure 2.11 shows the 10-minute chart at the time of the four-hour trend wall breakout. The vertical line shows the first time the ROI oscillator at the bottom of the chart crossed up to the right of the breakout. This is where the trade should be entered. This is the simple "drill-down" process. You can see to the right of the vertical line that profit was realized very quickly. You can also see where the previous support was for the stop-loss value.

In the following figures you will find 10 more trades indicated when the market comes close to a trend wall. Each one is numbered sequentially.

Entries 2 and 3 are shown with vertical lines on the following example in Figure 2.11. There is an oscillation between them where the ROI crossed

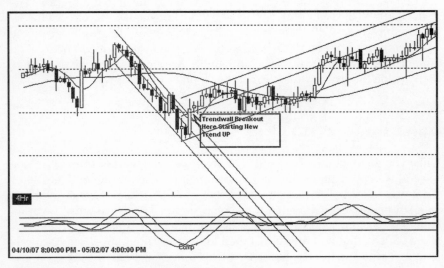

FIGURE 2.10 Four-Hour Trend Wall Breakout
Source: Copyright © 2007, Concorde Forex Group, Inc.

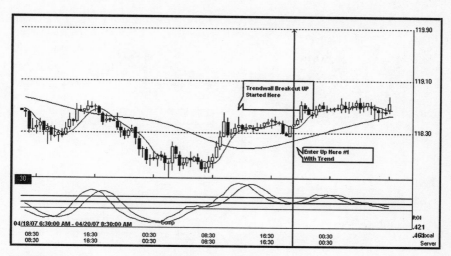

FIGURE 2.11 10-Minute Chart View of Breakout
Source: Copyright © 2007, Concorde Forex Group, Inc.

up, but no entry is indicated. This is because the time of the ROI cross
was between the London and Tokyo markets where the Forex is less reliable. During this period of time, the market typically is not moving and the
oscillators reload and move toward a neutral position. The time shown on
these examples is Eastern time. It is clear that both of these entries were
following a low point on the chart. This is because they occur right after
the market has come close to the four-hour trend wall bottom line. Isn't
that simple?

Notice to the right of trade number 3 (in Figure 2.12) that the ROI
crossed up, but no entry was made. This is because the market was not
close to the four-hour trend wall. There might be other reasons to make
this trade, but for our purposes here we are limiting our trading to one
specific condition.

Figure 2.13 shows two additional trades after the market comes close
to the four-hour bottom trend wall. Remember that we are trading only
with the trend in this example, so we are ignoring any market moves toward the upper trend wall. The risk we are taking here is that ultimately
there will be a breakout on the downside where no bounce will develop.
But, if we wait for a 10-minute ROI cross up, then the breakout should occur when we are not in the market. If you refer back to the four-hour chart,
you will notice that a breakout on the downside did occur twice during the
course of the uptrend. In the following example, you will notice that there
is a bold vertical line where the breakout occurred.

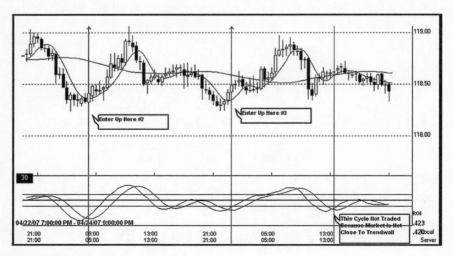

FIGURE 2.12 Trades 2 and 3
Source: Copyright © 2007, Concorde Forex Group, Inc.

The breakout signals the end of the uptrend and the beginning of a new downtrend. We, therefore, change our interest at this point to trading down instead of trading up. As we drill-down to the 10-minute chart you will notice there is another vertical line showing the ROI oscillator crossing down to the right of the bold vertical line. This is the entry point for the trade going down. You can see that the move down did not last very long,

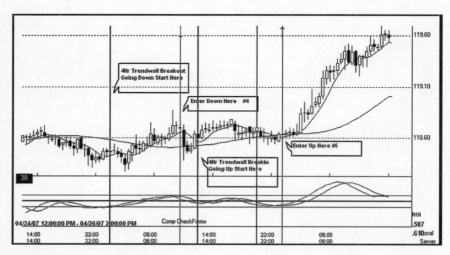

FIGURE 2.13 Trades 4 and 5
Source: Copyright © 2007, Concorde Forex Group, Inc.

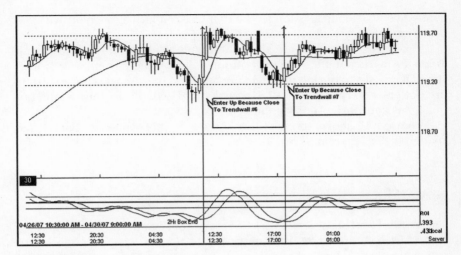

FIGURE 2.14 Trades 6 and 7
Source: Copyright © 2007, Concorde Forex Group, Inc.

and it did not go very far. But, it did move more than 20 pips, which is an excellent trade.

Between trades four and five, you will see another vertical line indicating where the market returned back inside the four-hour trend wall. This is an indication that our trading direction should return back to the upside.

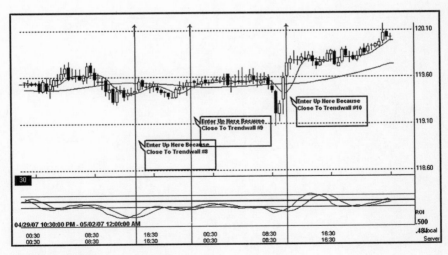

FIGURE 2.15 Final 3 Trades
Source: Copyright © 2007, Concorde Forex Group, Inc.

Trade five was made as soon as the ROI crossed into agreement with the direction that we want to trade.

Trades six and seven are shown in Figure 2.14 as the ROI crosses up when the market bounces off the bottom of the four-hour trend wall. Notice the ROI crosses to the left and right are not good trade entries because they are not close to the trend wall. Because of this condition, they would not qualify as appropriate entry points.

Figure 2.15 shows the final three trades in this sequence. Each trade rendered 10 or more pips profit.

SUMMARY

These trend wall observations are important for several reasons. First, they can be used to find good trade entry points. Second, they can be used to orient the trader during bad trades. For example, if I am in a trade and suffering a loss, one of the items on my checklist is to look at the anatomy of the medium and large time compression trend walls. If I am near the upper trend wall with a trade going down, I might wait for the upper trend wall to be reached and then enter a second trade down with more lots. When the two trades have a net positive position, both trades can then be closed with overall profit. This is the process called "cost averaging," and we will spend more time on this subject in Chapter 5.

CHAPTER 3

Convergence & Divergence

T he concept of convergence and divergence is very sensible as we look for subtle indications of changes in the trend. Another way of approaching this issue is to ask, "Is this trend running out of steam?" When the highs are getting higher, or lows are getting lower, we are encouraged to look for reasons to enter the market in that direction. But, when the highs are not getting higher, then sometimes it is an indication that a reversal is about to begin.

But, the Forex is so very dynamic that these convergence/divergence rules become very complicated. For example, I was studying a web site on this topic where the examples that were used had three sets of oscillators at the bottom of the chart. There were two separate Slow Stochastics and one MACD oscillator. Not only that, but there was a total of 16 lines in those oscillators. How am I ever going to understand and learn how to trade using 16 lines?

Even if I learn how to use 16 lines, I will then need to learn the differences between "regular divergence" and "hidden divergence," and the rules for trading just exceeded my ability.

My approach to divergence is very simple: If the oscillator is moving in the opposite direction of the chart candles or bars, then I have divergence. Period. In Figure 3.1, I have drawn three arrows to indicate the divergence where the 5-period and 20-period moving average lines are following the market and are moving in one direction while the MACD lines at the bottom of the chart are going in the opposite direction. If the trader waits for indicators to be convergent, some bad decisions can be avoided as the trend is followed in a precise manner.

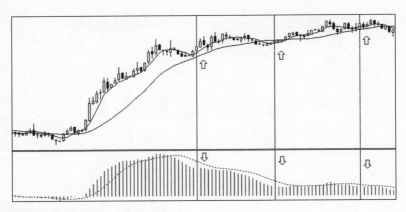

FIGURE 3.1   Divergence Example
Source: Copyright 2001–2007, MetaQuotes Software Corp.

Figure 3.2 shows four arrows where the market, moving averages, and oscillator at the bottom of the chart are convergent. These are clearly more productive market entry points. Isn't that simple? In this example I am ignoring the MACD oscillator in the lower section of the chart.

Figure 3.1 and Figure 3.2 are using a chart with the MACD oscillator set at 12, 26, and 9. The traditional use of the MACD is to compare the sequential highs and the sequential lows of the oscillator to see if they are getting higher or lower. Unfortunately, the Forex is so dynamic that by the time the oscillator reflects the market move, that market move could already be completed causing the trader to enter a trade in the wrong direction. To the

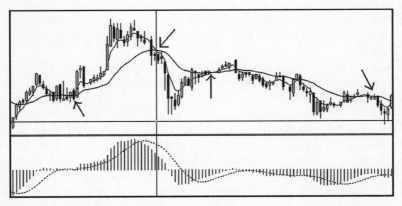

FIGURE 3.2   MACD
Source: Copyright 2001–2007, MetaQuotes Software Corp.

left of the vertical line, the highs are higher and the lows are higher telling us that the market is going up and getting stronger. But, by the time you draw that conclusion, the move up is over. Now, that was not much help. To the right of the vertical line the MACD lows are slightly lower and the highs are flat while the market is going down leaving us to wait to enter the market. This is typical Forex behavior. The retracements are so severe, that it throws the technical trader in the wrong direction, or causes the trader to wait and do nothing.

Let's look at some other data with a Slow Stochastics oscillator set at 12, 26, and 9. Notice in the middle of Figure 3.3 there is a period of time where the market is going up while the oscillator is going down. This is a simple divergence that is easy to identify and utilize. The way that I use this information is to consider the market to be primary, while the oscillator is secondary. The oscillator divergence is demonstrating a weakness, but when it is going down while the market is going up, it is reloading to be in position for the next market surge upward with the trend. Quite often, but not always, the surge following a "reload" like this is significant.

Notice to the right of the divergence where the oscillator fast line crossed the slow line going up. This is usually the point to enter the market going with the trend.

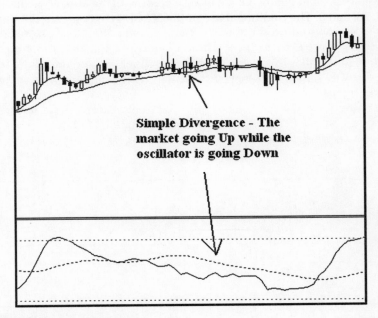

Simple Divergence – The market going Up while the oscillator is going Down

FIGURE 3.3 Slow Stochastic
Source: Copyright 2001–2007, MetaQuotes Software Corp.

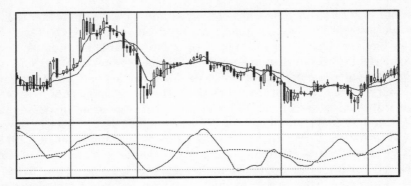

FIGURE 3.4 Slow Stochastic
Source: Copyright 2001–2007, MetaQuotes Software Corp.

The above divergence is easy to work with and utilize. I like it. This does not happen every day, and it is just one of the patterns that I look for. So, I do not bother with the 16 oscillating lines on my chart. I work with just four, and it is very manageable.

Moving back to the original example, I will show how the Stochastic oscillator is used under normal trading conditions in the search for convergence. Notice each of the vertical lines represents the moment in time where all four lines are moving in the same direction. Figure 3.4 is a beautiful picture showing how a trader can take advantage of market momentum at the simplest level. The left-most line is where the trader would enter up. The middle two lines are entries down, while the right-most line is an entry up.

Figure 3.5 is another illustration that demonstrates how most oscillators can be used. This is the "standard deviation" indicator using a 20 data point setting. Notice how the convergences effectively point to a good

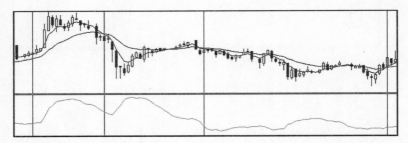

FIGURE 3.5 Standard Deviation
Source: Copyright 2001–2007, MetaQuotes Software Corp.

market entry with the trend. The vertical lines are placed approximately in the same position as the other oscillators in the previous examples for the same data. An entry point is determined by the convergence of all the lines without consideration of which line is last to come into agreement with the other two. The left-most vertical line shows the point where the oscillator becomes more angled upward. The next two lines to the right show the points where the slow-moving average line turns downward in agreement with the other two lines. The right-most vertical line shows where both the slow-moving average and the oscillator come into agreement upward with the moving average fast line. This is a 15-minute chart of the USD/JPY currency pair covering a little over 24 hours.

Figure 3.6 is another example of convergence using the Relative Vigor Index with the period setting of 10. Again we wait for the four lines to come into agreement to enter a trade. In this example there is a loss shown by the third vertical line for the trade that would be entered down at that point. That loss going down is easily recovered with the entry going up to its right.

As you have seen in the Figures 3.1 through 3.6, the issue of convergence and divergence can be utilized to your advantage with most technical oscillators. Looking for and identifying these entry points can be very profitable. All of the examples in this chapter are from the USD/JPY currency pair with the 15-minute chart period. You will find that some charting time

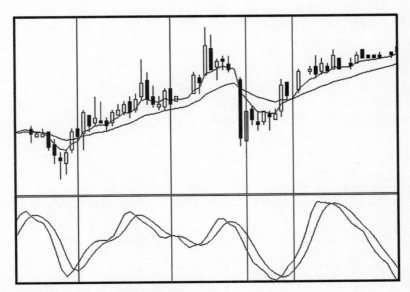

FIGURE 3.6 Relative Vigor Index
Source: Copyright 2001–2007, MetaQuotes Software Corp.

interval periods do not correlate well, and have very few convergent points, while others work quite well. For example, the four-hour chart might go days without convergence points using these oscillators.

SUMMARY

It is important to note that technical trading is more effective when the market is active. Cross currencies that involve Old and New World or Far Eastern countries begin to become more active when the Tokyo market opens daily, and become inactive when the London market closes. Cross currencies involving New World countries only become active about the middle of the London market, and become inactive when the London market closes.

CHAPTER 4

The Bad Trade

A technical approach to trading presumes market behavior will be consistent. This presumption is often correct if the trader is willing to interpret the technical indicators with great precision. But, when this is done the number of trades actually entered is severely limited. Seasoned traders have learned that the "Ratio of Winning Trades" curve has diminishing returns. That is to say, a good trader with some failures will make much more profit than a trader who waits only for perfect technical patterns, because so few perfect patterns occur. Therefore, it seems safe to say that all traders, even good ones, experience and expect losses.

WHY AM I LOSING?

If good traders suffer losses, then how do they minimize the damage? The answer to this question is, first of all, dependent upon the reason for the loss.

Here are the basic reasons for losses:

- Bad Entry
- Bad Stop-Loss Value
- Bad Profit Limit Value
- News Announcement

Bad Entry

There are so many ways that one can enter bad trades, that I am not going to attempt to list them. One of the most frustrating things that we do as traders is make mistakes at the point of entry. For example, most traders have pressed the wrong button on the broker dealing station and sold when intending to buy, or bought one currency when attempting to buy another. These things happen. When the market is moving quickly, and we feel the need to make a decision quickly, we are vulnerable to carelessness. Sometimes we make mistakes when we are distracted. I recall when one of my friends announced to a group of other traders that he currently had over 200 trades in a row with no losses. Just then someone approached him and asked a question that caused a distraction. The distraction occurred just as he was closing a trade, and it caused him to click the wrong button that resulted in a closed trade that was not yet profitable, thus ending his winning streak. I received a call two days ago from my sister asking me to help her because her computer was not running. I told her not to worry, and I used my demo dealing station to log into her mini account. A good trade opportunity arrived, and I decided to help her and proceeded to enter a trade. I was hurried because the market was not standing still, and I forgot to doublecheck the number of lots before pressing the submit button. Instead of entering two lots, I mistakenly entered 20! Imagine how shocked I was a little while later when I discovered my error. It is a good thing that I was trading in the right direction, or there would have been a lot of stress while that trade was still open. There is nothing I can write in this paragraph to change your behavior under these conditions. So, we both struggle with this issue. Using a checklist is helpful, and I recommend it, as it forces us to consider all of the salient factors before entering a trade.

Bad Stop-Loss Value

In Chapter 1 the "Trader Audit," which describes the process of measuring the effectiveness of stop-loss values, was discussed. If you do not remember it, please turn back and review it again. This is a critical exercise for each and every trader to perform. You must be in a position to rate yourself on this issue: Are you good or bad at it? If you are good at it, then your bad trades are caused by entries in the wrong direction or at the wrong time. If you are bad at it, then you probably have problems in both areas.

There is a constant tension between the need to limit losses and the need to allow the market to move up and down for no apparent reason while a trade is open. If a trade is going to fail, then let's cut our losses quickly, right? This is very difficult to manage while the market is moving.

Quite often the Forex will return to test the previous support level before moving to the next target. So, if the stop loss value is moved prematurely, the trade will be closed with a loss or a small gain before the market moves to the target. From one moment to the next, who can tell what the Forex will do?

Most traders look left to see the previous support level that the Forex established and then set the stop-loss value somewhere just below that level. This seems reasonable, and it usually works. I find myself almost never setting a stop-loss value less than 15 pips, and seldom set one above 90 pips. My profit targets are typically between 15 and 50 pips, which set the stage for smaller stop-loss values. For traders who are making entries based upon the larger time compressions, and who are working with larger profit targets, a larger stop loss value is indicated. Those traders also look at the larger compressions to determine previous support points. Figure 4.1 demonstrates two support points to the left of the place where the trader is making a decision. The market to the right of the decision point continued to move upward without retracing back to the support points.

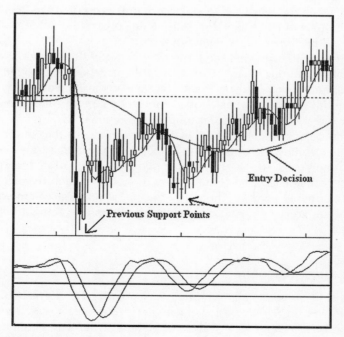

FIGURE 4.1 Support Points
Source: Copyright © 2007, Concorde Forex Group, Inc.

Bad Profit Limit Value

The Forex movement is driven by economic announcements. A trading day with no announcements is usually less dynamic, with moderate movement as the trading session progresses. Those days are typically driven by the last announcement and perhaps anticipation of the next one. One of the most common mistakes that a day-trader makes is anticipating a large market move when there is no economic news to drive it. There are many websites that list the dates and times for economic news releases, and the trader should always be aware of the news release schedule.

I have mixed feelings about entering a trade just prior to an announcement as the market might move swiftly against my trade, but on the other hand, quite often the technical indicators are excellent predictors of what effect the announcement will have on the market.

My rule of thumb for setting the profit target is 15 pips for most trades and 30-plus pips for trades with extra support from larger time compressions. By the time the market goes more than 20 pips on most moves, it oscillates multiple times and smaller entries for less pips can capture a fair share of the larger move with a much lower risk. I have observed many instances where I attempted to capture more than 30 pips, only to settle for 5 or less when the market retraced and hit my stop that had been moved to keep from avoiding a loss. Appendix A demonstrates the high value that just 10 pips profit per day accumulates.

Traders who are using the large time compressions, such as the day chart, will, of course, have much larger profit targets. But, if you look back at the market movement, you will usually see on the smaller time compressions multiple entries and exits that represent a larger profit potential. So, I prefer to work with the smaller time compressions.

While talking about profits, let me also point out that many traders make the mistake of setting goals. I think this is a huge mistake when dealing with the Forex. It is better to maintain an attitude of just taking what the Forex offers each day. Good traders do not manufacture trades. Good traders just avoid entering the market at the wrong time. Some days the Forex offers great opportunities, while on others it is fraught with extra danger.

News Announcements

In the previous section I described this process for the scheduled announcements. In addition to the scheduled announcements, there is always the issue of emergency announcements. When catastrophes strike, the market responds very rapidly. During these times the market makers are not sure what to do, and the market can swing wildly up and down.

In these instances there is no such thing as a technical interpretation, and Fibonacci ratios are ignored. Usually, however, order is restored within an hour, and trading can be resumed as before.

DECISIONS

When a trade is going badly, it is very difficult to decide what to do. At that point in time, there is an emotional investment in the trade that plays an important role. It is bad enough that there is a monetary loss at stake, but our reaction to the situation also rears its ugly head.

Traders with a high success rate might be able to shrug off the situation, and I suspect that they will never read this book. So I am talking with as much clarity that I can muster to help you in this undesirable situation. There are four choices: (1) let the market continue to move and hope for a return, (2) kill the trade and take the loss, (3) hedge the trade (enter another one in the opposite direction), (4) or move the stop. I don't know about you but the "hoping for return" method has not worked for me. I much prefer the other three options.

Killing the trade not only stops the bleeding, but it also releases the emotional attachment to the trade. In this situation I try to maintain my attachment and look for a way to get even. If you kill the trade and then pretend that you are still in the trade, and look for opportunities to enter in your previous direction for small incremental gains, the loss can be recovered over time. This affords me great satisfaction. Oh yes, if I can recover a loss in the same currency pair, it is a wonderful thing. This is the process of "cost averaging" that we will talk more about a little later.

Taking the loss is immediate and ruthless. It is also very painful not only because you lost money, but also because you are admitting that you are wrong and that the bankers, and every other trader in the world, is right. Whew, that was hard to say. If you want to move on and forget the whole painful experience, this is, sometimes, the best course of action.

Hedging is a tricky business. If after you bought a currency pair the market goes down, you always have the option of entering another trade in the new direction. If you are sure that the move will go down 20 pips against the first trade, and you enter the "sell" transaction with more lots than the original trade going up, and you set a profit limit of 10 pips, then the loss going down is mitigated by the profit of the second trade. But, if you are wrong, and you enter the second trade just before the market bounces back, then you will be in a worse situation with a bad trade with more lots at risk. There is also pain if the market moves somewhere between the two trades and taunts you. It will stay there until you are convinced that you have two bad trades. Hedging can become very stressful, so it is best to reserve its use for specific conditions that you know have a high rate of success.

Moving a stop-loss value is always a temptation when a trade starts to go bad. Most professional managers who trade the major currencies do not enter stop-loss values. This really surprised me when I learned about it, but I believe that they do it to make sure that the broker and banker are not tempted to force the market to that level and grab their position in the market. This is a very poor practice because you never know when some announcement will move the market 200 pips or more.

The most frequent time that I am tempted to move a stop-loss value is when a trade is moving the wrong way. Sometimes there are resistance points every 20 pips as the trade continues to move against me. These resistance points are incrementally deceptive, as I am convinced that the next one will turn the market. So, it is tempting to move the stop-loss value to the next resistance point in the hopes that the market will retrace at that point.

Good traders become very disciplined about moving stop-loss values, and they seldom do it. Let the loss occur, and have the confidence that it can be recovered with the next few trades. I will cost average a trade that ended in failure — a topic that will be reviewed in detail later in this chapter.

TRENDS

The typical bad trade occurs because the trader enters against the trend. This cause far outweighs all others for the beginning trader. The majority of traders measure the trend with the use of moving averages. There are a number of settings to select from, but the concept is the same. Let's assume that past behavior will have some correlation to future behavior. My studies have shown that the five-candle moving average is an accurate predictor for the next data point only 41 percent of the time. For example, if five candlesticks on a five-minute chart are higher than the previous five candlesticks (shifted left one position), then the odds of the next candle being white (meaning going up in agreement with the moving average) are only 41 percent. I can already hear the mathematicians saying that there is, therefore, a 59 percent probability that the market will go down. Yes, but how much? The point I am making is that any one indicator on any one chart is not adequate. There is no simple way to use moving averages to predict future Forex behavior. The only way to do it is to compare the

moving averages for different time compressions. But, that is also difficult. For example, the correlation of the five-minute candles going in the
direction of the two-hour moving average is also about 41 percent accurate. When you add multiple time compressions together you begin to see
the correlation rise. For example, when you have agreement with the five-
minute, 10-minute, 30-minute and 60-minute moving averages, then the correlation does increase to help the trader. But, the process becomes very
complicated.

The moving averages on the medium and large time compression are
quite helpful as a general guide to define a trend. Once the trader decides
to use specific criteria for the trend decision, that same criteria should continue to be used until the trade is closed. This sounds easy, but when there
are conflicting indicators the trader can become confused or lose confidence in the one that was selected. For example, if the two-hour moving
average is going up and the four-hour moving average is going down, then
the trader needs to select the one over the other and stick with it. Quite
often, however, when this condition exists, it is best to wait for agreement to occur. When agreement is finally achieved as a result of one large
candle, it is difficult to make good trades when the majority of the candles
are retracing against the trend. The Forex frequently moves the market in
one direction with a lot of small candles, and then reverses the direction
and movement with a few large ones. The market behavior in one direction
is usually different than the behavior in the other one.

Let me show you what I mean in the four-hour chart example in
Figure 4.2. Notice that there are 31 candlesticks in this little down trend,
and that there are four candlesticks that represent most of the movement
down, while the rest of the candlesticks either are against the trend, or are
somewhat flat. This illustrates the challenges that face the Forex trader.
If this data is parsed more precisely, then we will see that there are really three different trends in this example. Following the fast-moving average line, we will notice a trend down (starting five candles from the left),
a trend up (starting with candle 11) and finally another trend back down
(starting to the right of the large black candle in the center). After the first
candlestick down (number 5), the market begins moving up, but the moving average doesn't turn until the move up is nearly over. The next move
down occurs while the moving average is telling us to keep going up, and
so on. This illustration helps us to understand the extra value that the trend
walls add. Following the moving averages puts us behind the market where
we are unable to make profit. We need to use tools that also show market
anticipation. Notice how the trend walls affected the market.

While moving averages are good to use, I prefer to use them with the
trend wall tool because it encompasses the moving average as well as

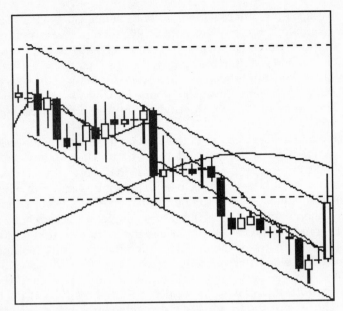

FIGURE 4.2 Moving Average Trend vs. Trend Walls
Source: Copyright © 2007, Concorde Forex Group, Inc.

demonstrates the trading channel. Over the past six years I have found that this is a challenge for most traders. It seems that most traders cannot understand the importance of drawing trend walls. Hopefully the examples that I am showing in this book are making an impression on your mind.

The trend is a critical component of a trade because it needs to be depended upon for profit, and if a retracement occurs before profits are realized then it needs to be depended upon to bring the market back for recovery.

I cannot stress this enough. This is critical for successful trading, because I believe that if a trader cannot "cost average" then a trader cannot succeed. If you are trading against the trend, then cost averaging cannot work. If you are trading against the trend, then the second (cost average) trade will just add to the loss.

If a trade is entered against the trend, the only remedy at that point is to hedge and trade the other way to the next resistance point in the market. When the resistance point is reached, the second trade is closed for profit, and then another trade can be considered in the direction of the original trade.

RETRACEMENTS

By definition, every market move is followed by a retracement. The concept is simple enough, but in practice it is very difficult to utilize. The Forex does not conform to predefined standards as it moves wildly from one point to another. The difficulty is not whether there will be a retracement. The difficulty is determining when and how much. When we are caught in a bad trade it is helpful to look at different time compressions to see if the market is in the middle of a retracement. If it appears that a retracement has started, then we are able to assess the potential profit and loss. It is helpful to keep in mind that market surges and retracements begin with news announcements, when Tokyo, London, or New York markets prepare to open, and two hours before the London market closes. If I am in trouble at 9:50 a.m. Eastern time, I will wait to see if the market changes direction between 10:00 and 10:30 a.m. before closing a losing position. The first 15 days of each month are when the major monthly announcements are made by each country, and are, therefore, usually much more volatile. It is less certain if the market will trend in one direction or if it will reverse itself wildly each day. The second half of each month is different because the market is trying to anticipate, and position itself for the impending announcements in the next month. It is easier for beginning traders to trade the second half of the month as a result.

SUMMARY

Let's face it; there are too many ways to make a bad trade, and there are too few ways to recover. If you want to salvage a bad trade, then you will:

1. Determine the trend and then recover only in that direction.
2. Either wait and enter a cost average trade at a resistance point, and then enter another trade on the retracement.
3. Hedge the loser to a resistance point.

The next chapter describes in more detail the "cost average" process.

CHAPTER 5

Bad Trade
Recovery

I n the previous chapters, bad trade recovery was introduced and placed in the proper context for a clear understanding, but it was not fully described. So, in this chapter we will take a much closer look at the details. Cost averaging is typically used when a trade is in a negative condition and the trader is attempting to minimize the loss or make an overall gain. You might wonder why we don't just wait for the loss condition to occur before entering any trade and then just enter the cost average trade to minimize risk. I would agree that this is an option, except so many initial trades that work would be untraded that the overall profits would be less.

As previously stated, it is critical to invoke this process only in the direction of the trend. If the original trade is not in the direction of the trend, then this process can be followed as a hedge, which will be with the trend and against the initial trade direction.

This process cannot be invoked at any point, but must be invoked at a point where the market is most likely to reverse course. If a buy transaction is entered at 1.2500 and the market drops to 1.2450, an arbitrary number should not be used. The trader must determine a technical reason to conclude that the retracement has ended and an appropriate time to enter a second trade upward has arrived. A friend of mine who attempted to cost average using an arbitrary method lost 75 percent of his account overnight. He was entering another cost average trade whenever the market went against him 50 or more pips. It was a stressful and expensive lesson for him to learn. Some traders use the "envelope" method, which is the average number of pips that a specific currency pair moves at a time. For example, the EUR/USD typically moves 25-30 pips, then moves sideways, or moves another 25-30 pips. This information sounds helpful, but it is unreliable when it comes to trading. The best method for me to locate these points of reversal is to use the River Oscillator Indicator (ROI) that is described in more detail later in this chapter. In subsequent chapters, I will demonstrate how to accomplish the same thing with several other oscillators and trend lines.

I have discovered that the key to success is to reference two time compressions that have a ratio between 8:1 and 12:1. For example, if I use the 10-minute chart with the two-hour chart, or the 30-minute chart with the four-hour chart, or the two-hour chart with the day chart, the market harmonics allow the trader to make decisions using the market oscillations more effectively. When working with these ratios the various oscillating tools seem to work better. I have not tried to determine why these work, but have just accepted them and use them to my advantage.

Let me illustrate first with the combination of the day chart and the two-hour chart for the USD/CAD. This illustration and most of the previous illustrations are using the SmartCharts™, which is a product used by Concorde Forex Group, Inc. (CFG). These charts utilize a proprietary oscillator called the River Oscillator Indicator or ROI. I prefer these charts for three reasons. First, they are used by my good friend and colleague Donald Snellgrove, who runs CFG that mentors Forex traders. They have repeatedly demonstrated that their method of trading with this oscillator is capable of generating large numbers of successful trades with few losses. I believe the record held by one trader is over 400 trades with no losses. If you know anything about the Forex, then you understand just how incredible this is. When most experienced Forex traders hear of this record, they refuse to believe it. There is a copy of the trading history for an account that Don traded in his book *Selective Trading: How to Achieve over 100 Trades in a Row without a Loss*, published by John Wiley & Sons, Inc., 2008.

The ROI oscillator is a miracle, and none of us know why it works. I was commissioned by Don Snellgrove in 2001 to develop a chart product, and he contracted with a large data supplier for the data feed. At that time he was comfortable with another product, and thought that he might be able to license the oscillator that he had been working with for several years. But, when I was ready for the formula, he had not yet contacted the firm, so I developed the ROI and worked with it for a few days before presenting it to him for further testing. He soon discovered that it was a magnificent oscillator, and the rest is history. So, even though I developed it in just a few days, I still consider it to be a miracle. I must point out that for any oscillator to work, the market must be moving to allow the oscillator lines to establish angle and separation. When the market is moving in a very tight range, it is much more difficult to determine where and when it will move next.

DAY AND TWO HOUR

In any event, here is a day chart illustration. The chart shown in Figure 5.1 contains only a portion of the data, and does not show the values for the horizontal dashed lines or the values for any candlestick data. What we are interested in is the oscillator lines as they cross up and down. I have drawn eight vertical lines with arrows at the top of each line showing the direction that should be traded to the right of each line. A trade is not blindly entered at this point, but using the 12:1 ratio (12 two-hour periods in each day), we will examine the data on the two-hour chart beginning at the date/time of the vertical line on the day chart. Moving from a larger time compression to a smaller one is called "drilling down." This data includes the time period of Jan. 11 – Feb. 5, 2007, for the USD/CAD currency combination. I selected this example because it includes a variety of market conditions. It begins with a market with tentative moves down and up, followed by moves that are a little more demonstrative, and ending with a large trending market. As I have stated before, any system of trading can succeed during a trending market. The real test is to measure the results of the non-trending market and the market during a transition from trending to non-trending patterns.

Notice that to the right of each ROI cross (the oscillator on the bottom of the chart) the market does not always move in the expected direction. In some cases, the market starts in the wrong direction and then changes to follow the ROI direction, while in other cases, it never comes into agreement. We will examine each of these areas on the two-hour chart below.

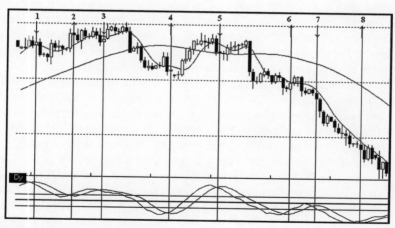

FIGURE 5.1 Day Chart Oscillations
Source: Copyright © 2007, Concorde Forex Group, Inc.

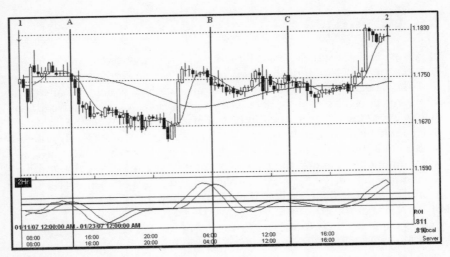

FIGURE 5.2 Two-Hour Data
Source: Copyright © 2007, Concorde Forex Group, Inc.

Figure 5.2 contains a picture of the two-hour data between vertical lines 1 and 2 from the day chart. Throughout this chapter, you might need to refer back to Figure 5.1 as we drill down to the two-hour chart for each change in direction.

To the right of the vertical line number 1 there are three oscillations where the ROI fast line crosses the ROI slow line downward. Each of these three oscillations are lettered A-C. The values to the right of the chart give us an idea of the number of pips that each one moved. It is clear that each one of these oscillations (A, B and C) was quite profitable as we take advantage of the 12:1 ratio. To the right of vertical line 2, we will begin to look for trades upward as shown in the next figure below.

This process is utilized when a "bad trade" has been entered somewhere between these points, but in the direction of the trend. The trader must then wait for the ROI to cross or re-cross in the appropriate direction and then enter the second trade, which is "cost averaging." This process can also be utilized to determine the best time to enter the first trade.

Notice in Figure 5.3, the vertical lines D-G where the ROI oscillator crossed up. Line D would have been a loss of approximately 20 pips if the trader had exited the trade when the oscillator leveled off, or started moving in the down direction. Trade entries at Lines E-G would have been quite profitable. Because we are using the large time compressions, the stop-loss value would be correspondingly larger than if we were trading with the five-minute chart.

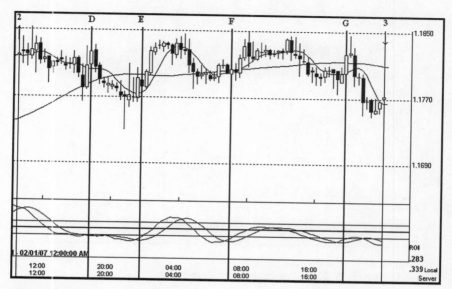

FIGURE 5.3 Two-Hour Chart (D-G)
Source: Copyright © 2007, Concorde Forex Group, Inc.

Figure 5.4 shows the next two oscillations in agreement with the day chart.

Lines H and I show the next two profitable entries downward as the ROI oscillator crosses in agreement with the direction of vertical line number 3.

Figure 5.5 shows the next oscillations in the same direction.

Vertical lines J-M show the entries downward. Notice that entries L and M would not have rendered profits, but would have been minor losers. This is a good time to point out that the best entries typically follow a market surge in the other direction. Some traders would, therefore, state that these are all retracement trades, and I will not debate that point. But, this is a good time to go back and review all 13 trades (A-M) and examine the entries where the market surges just prior to the vertical entry lines.

Figure 5.6 shows the next moves as indicated by vertical line 5 on the day chart.

Notice, again, the success offered by this methodology, as shown by vertical lines N-R. To the right of vertical line N, the direction shifts up, and lines O-R show the entries. The toughest test of any technical trading system is determined by its ability to make the transition from a trending market to an oscillating market. In these examples, you can easily see how it is successfully making this important transition.

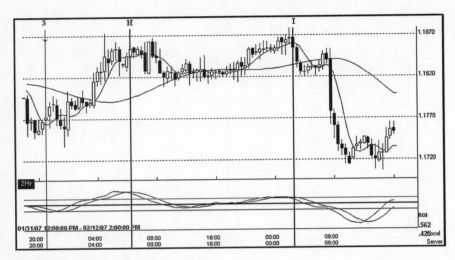

FIGURE 5.4 Two-Hour Chart (H-I)
Source: Copyright © 2007, Concorde Forex Group, Inc.

Figure 5.7 shows the remaining movies upward to the right of vertical line 5.

In these examples, you can see to the right of vertical line T there was a minor loss, but it was also not preceded by a surge going down and back up.

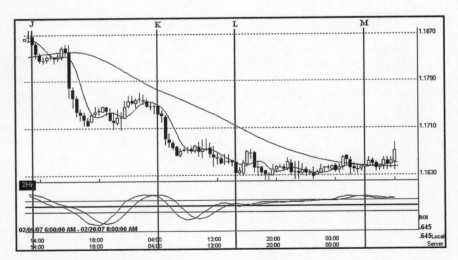

FIGURE 5.5 Two-Hour Chart (J-M)
Source: Copyright © 2007, Concorde Forex Group, Inc.

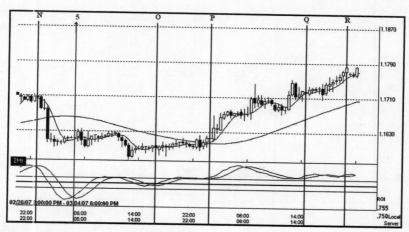

FIGURE 5.6 Two-Hour Chart (N-R)
Source: Copyright © 2007, Concorde Forex Group, Inc.

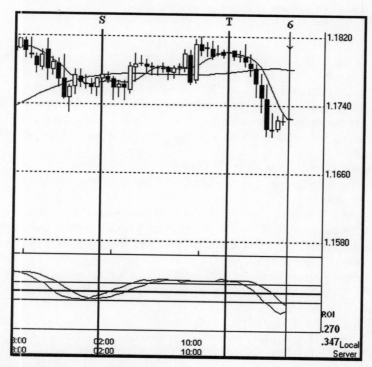

FIGURE 5.7 Two-Hour Chart (R-V)
Source: Copyright © 2007, Concorde Forex Group, Inc.

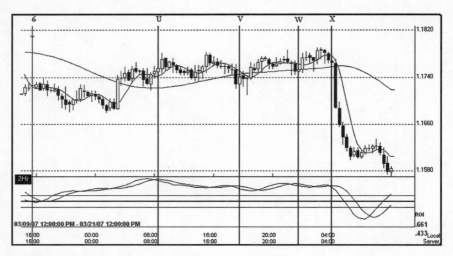

FIGURE 5.8 Two-Hour Chart (W-AB)
Source: Copyright © 2007, Concorde Forex Group, Inc.

Figure 5.8 shows the next moves downward to the right of vertical line 6.

There are small losses on the entries for vertical lines U and W, but the profit for entry X more than makes up for it. Did you notice that these losses are not preceded by a surge? Just compare the chart patterns U and V to understand what I am looking for with the surge to the left of the vertical line.

Figure 5.9 shows the next cycle up.

The entry to the right of line Y would have a small loss, but the others look very healthy.

Figure 5.10 shows cycle 7. I hope that your eyes are not glazing over yet. If you are having difficulty in following all of this detailed information, I suggest that you use a pencil and make notes and draw your own arrows and notes on these charts.

These are probably the least profitable trades we have seen so far. This was a very short up cycle on the day chart, and you can see line 8 begins our last cycle down.

Figure 5.11 shows our last cycle down.

The vertical lines demonstrate the value of the 12:1 ratio when using the ROI oscillator. This might be a tedious exercise, but when you begin to use these techniques, you will want to see plenty of examples. At least I always do. Vertical line 8 begins an up cycle on the day chart during a steep

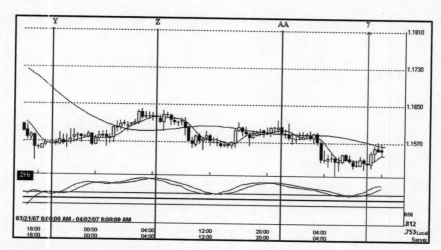

FIGURE 5.9 Two-Hour Chart (Y-AA)
Source: Copyright © 2007, Concorde Forex Group, Inc.

down market. These divergent conditions are difficult to trade, and I will have plenty of advice for you to consider later on.

As you review the examples for this selected time frame of Jan. 11 – Feb. 5, 2007, it is easy to see the benefits derived from this technique. In the following chapters I will use both to demonstrate this important technique.

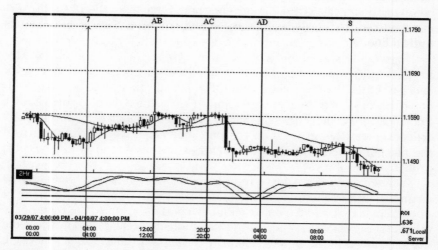

FIGURE 5.10 Two-Hour Chart (AB-AD)
Source: Copyright © 2007, Concorde Forex Group, Inc.

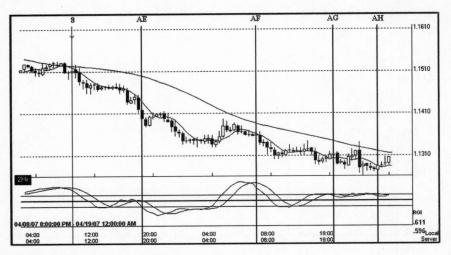

FIGURE 5.11 Two-Hour Chart (AE-AH)
Source: Copyright © 2007, Concorde Forex Group, Inc.

ONE HOUR AND FIVE MINUTE

The previous example used the day and two-hour chart combination. Now, let me show a similar comparison using the one-hour and five-minute chart combination for the EUR/USD currency pair. Remember the 12:1 ratio? Remember also that these trade entry points are used when a cost average trade is needed. Experienced traders also use them for initial entries.

Figure 5.12 shows the one-hour ROI crosses for May 10–16, 2007, for the EUR/USD currency pair. This example is being selected with no prior analysis other than the good trade that I made today as the euro went down. Because of this very nice example (see to the right of vertical line 6), I decided to use this currency pair to demonstrate a little history as well. Whenever the ROI crosses on the one-hour chart we will drill down to the five-minute chart and look for entries in that direction for five pips profit.

You will probably want to refer back to Figure 5.12 as the subsequent examples drill down to the five-minute chart for trade entries. To the right of vertical lines 1 and 6 the market moved perfectly, but to the right of the others there was divergence as the ROI indicated one direction while the market moved in the other. This proves the point that no charting oscillator is always perfect. The key to success is to drill down to the smaller compressions to find opportunities as they are presented in the direction that you want.

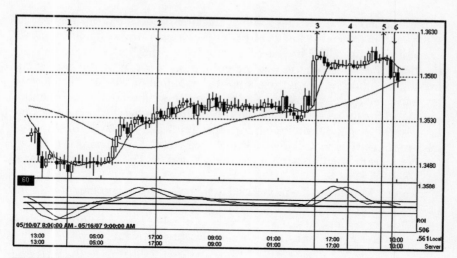

FIGURE 5.12 One-Hour Chart
Source: Copyright © 2007, Concorde Forex Group, Inc.

Figure 5.13 shows our first look at this sequence using the five-minute chart. Because of the smaller time compression, notice that the horizontal lines on the chart delineate smaller values. In this example, they are only 20 pips between each horizontal line. The technical stop-loss value for the trade entry on vertical line A is less than 10 pips, which for the Forex

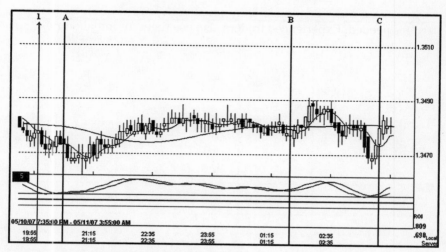

FIGURE 5.13 Five-Minute Chart (A-C)
Source: Copyright © 2007, Concorde Forex Group, Inc.

is unreasonable. I drew line A when the ROI crossed up, but there is no separation between the lines until after the market dropped a little further and bounced up. This little surge downward is what I look for to indicate the best time to enter the market going up. Because of the use of the five-minute chart, my profit expectations are smaller, and are usually just five pips per trade. Quite often, a trade on this time compression builds and develops an identical trade on the 10-minute chart, which allows me to keep the original trade going for more profit if I just wait for things to mature. Lines B and C show the next two trading opportunities. Notice the flat market conditions between lines A and B? The Tokyo market was quiet on this day.

Figure 5.14 shows the next three ROI crosses up in agreement with the one-hour chart direction.

The entries for lines D and F were profitable very quickly, while the entry for line E was not. In this example entry F would have developed before entry E was closed with profit. This would introduce for the trader the need for a decision. Because the two entries are almost the same, I generally do not make the second entry unless it is 10 or more pips better than the first entry. This allows me to add lots and cost average my first entry. So, in this case, I would not enter where line F is drawn.

Figure 5.15 shows the market moving up to give us the profit for the entry that was made for line E.

Line 2 is drawn to show us the time that the one-hour chart ROI crosses down. This is the trigger for us to change our focus and begin to look for

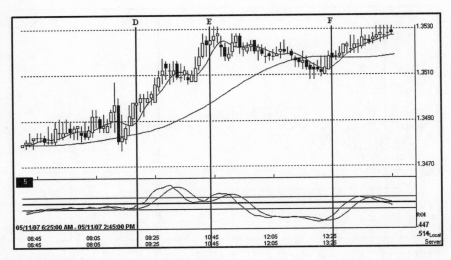

FIGURE 5.14   Five-Minute Chart (D-F)
Source: Copyright © 2007, Concorde Forex Group, Inc.

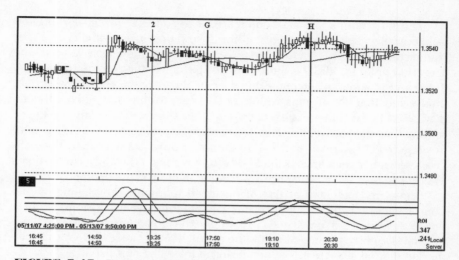

FIGURE 5.15 Five-Minute Chart (G-H)
Source: Copyright © 2007, Concorde Forex Group, Inc.

entries down. Lines G and H are both good entries down. The market dropped 12 pips to the right of line G, giving us room to realize a five pip profit.

Figure 5.16 shows the next three potential trade entries down as indicated by the one-hour chart ROI.

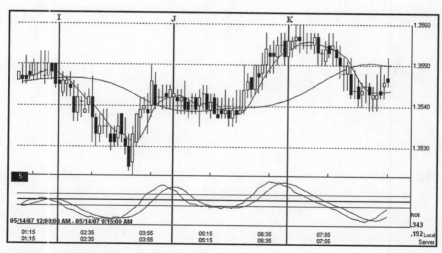

FIGURE 5.16 Five-Minute Chart (I-K)
Source: Copyright © 2007, Concorde Forex Group, Inc.

The entry points for lines I and K are clearly quick in profit. The market fell about eight pips to the right of line J, so there is a possibility that the trade would not have reached five pips profit before moving upward again. The entry point for line K is more than 10 pips above the entry point for line J, so I would add lots and enter down again at that point. Let me point out, once again, that my stop-loss value for the entry for line J would not be under 1.3560, but would probably be in the 1.3563-5 area. Either way, the entry for line K would recover any loss and provide opportunity for overall profit.

Figure 5.17 shows the next two entries downward. Notice the ROI cross down between lines L and M where I have not indicated a trade entry. This is because there is no surge preceding the ROI cross down.

The entry indicated at line M occurred following the closing of the London market, which usually begins a quiet period where the market does not move as much. We will need to examine the next figure to see what happened. The entry for line M would be about 1.3546, and it is clear that the market did fall close to 1.3530 rendering at least five pips profit.

Figure 5.18 shows the next two entries downward.

Line O, as you can see, is problematic. The market did not move downward to give us five pips profit. We will need to look at the next figure to determine the cost average trade required for this entry.

Figure 5.19 shows us why stops are so important. You might have been thinking that you could just leave a trade open, wait for the next entry, make the second entry, and then close both trades at the same time later when overall profit is achieved. But, here is an example of the technical

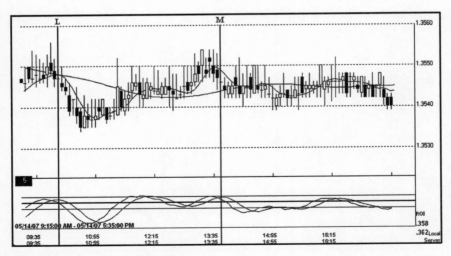

FIGURE 5.17 Five-Minute Chart (L-M)
Source: Copyright © 2007, Concorde Forex Group, Inc.

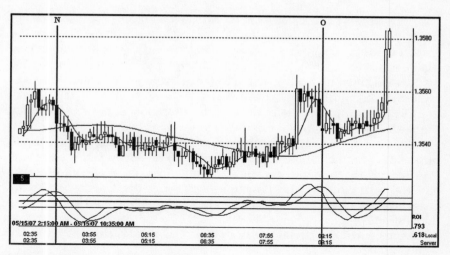

FIGURE 5.18 Five-Minute Chart (N-O)
Source: Copyright © 2007, Concorde Forex Group, Inc.

indicators telling us that the market overall direction has reversed course and is now going up. At this point in time, we could not know how far up it will go, so any open trades going down could be extremely risky. When working with the five-minute chart, I prefer to work with a stop-loss value around 15 pips. If my first entry is one lot and I lose 15 pips, then the second

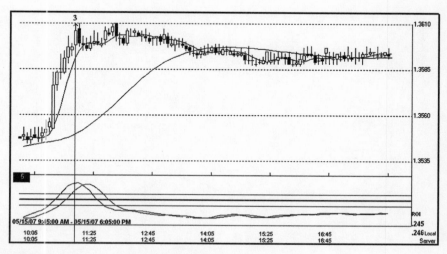

FIGURE 5.19 Five-Minute Chart (no entries)
Source: Copyright © 2007, Concorde Forex Group, Inc.

entry is four lots and I am looking for five pips profit, the result will be net profit of five pips. In the case of line O, we would just wait for a day for the market to provide us with the opportunity to recover from this minor loss. Again, this is an example of why I do not believe in goals. I have no goals, so I am not frustrated and tempted to try to make profits where the risks are higher than normal.

The market to the right of line 3 is the afternoon, so we must wait for the Tokyo market to open for more volatility.

Figure 5.20 shows us that the market is changing yet again back to the downside. Yes, this is just what we want it to do so we can recover our previous loss in the same direction. It really does not matter though. We can trade extra lots in either direction when recovering from a loss. In this case the entry on line P is approximately 1.3603 and did not render profits until after line Q.

Again, I would not enter at line Q because it is so close to the entry value for line P.

Figure 5.21 shows the market falling to give us the profit that we need for the cost average entry for line P. The value at line R is also very close to the value for line P, so I would not enter again until the previous trade is closed.

Just to the right of line 5, the market fell to give us the profit for the previous cost average trade going down. Line 5 signals the beginning of another change in direction, and line S would enter the market at about

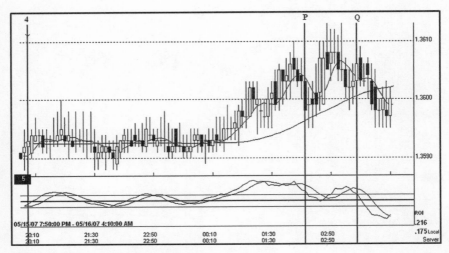

FIGURE 5.20 Five-Minute Chart (P-Q)
Source: Copyright © 2007, Concorde Forex Group, Inc.

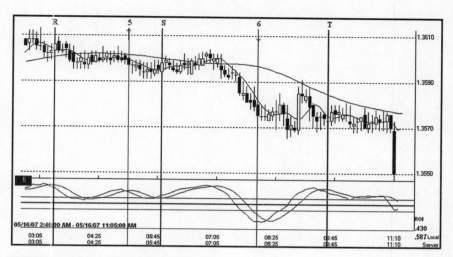

FIGURE 5.21 Five-Minute Chart (R-T)
Source: Copyright © 2007, Concorde Forex Group, Inc.

1.3594. The market moved upward to 1.3604, which would give us the five pips that we are seeking.

Line T indicates the entry I made that caused me to select this as an example to show you here. I entered down following the little surge upward, and waited for the market to fall. Sure enough, the Forex without notice moved quickly to meet my expected profit point.

SUMMARY

"Cost averaging" is the best way to recover from a "bad trade." Always utilize the stop-loss feature offered by the broker to minimize the overall risk of any one trade. Waiting for the next entry opportunity and increasing the number of lots will provide an opportunity to recover the previous loss as well as to make an additional profit. In the following chapters, you will see examples using various technical indicators from which you can select at any time to manage a "bad trade." The examples also use the "drill-down" technique from the day chart to the two-hour, one-hour or 30-minute charts. The examples also use the four-hour chart with the 30-minute charts.

CHAPTER 6

Loss Recovery with MACD

The figures in this chapter will be limited to trading the MACD crossovers only as shown for the GBP/USD currency combination. Chapter 9 demonstrates the use of moving averages, so it would be redundant to include them in this chapter. As you know, the MACD utilizes moving averages, and shows a trigger line that we will ignore at this time. The settings on these examples are 12, 26 and 9. Only the crossovers will be employed for this study. Figure 6.1 shows bold vertical lines where the crossovers occurred on the day chart during the summer of 2006. We will examine five of these crossovers that began in July and extended through September. In the previous chapter I discussed the "drill-down" technique using the day chart and the two-hour chart. In this study I am using the day chart and the 30-minute chart to demonstrate the versatility of the methodology.

These examples were chosen carefully to work with market conditions that are typical and not the best for trading. To the right of vertical line 1, the market did go up as expected, but to the right of line 2, the market continued to move up, while the MACD was telling us to trade down. To the right of line 3, the divergence continued as the market went down while the trader is lead to find trades going up. Section 4 is a mixture and will also provide some good illustrations.

The first crossover up on the day chart was on July 21, but the first crossover up on the 30-minute chart following was on July 25 at 9:30, and it was not successful by my standards. The entry to the right of vertical line A, as shown in Figure 6.2, would have been approximately 1.8514 and offered about 10 pips profit before dramatically retracing. This is an interesting

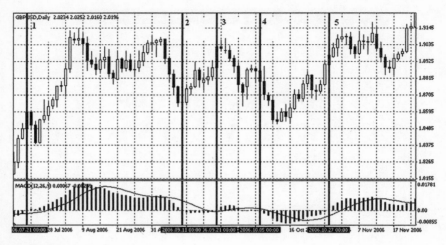

FIGURE 6.1   Day Chart Trends
Source: Copyright 2001–2007, MetaQuotes Software Corp.

condition as the first support to the left of the entry is more than 60 pips away. It is typical to use large stop-loss settings when working with these time compressions. The stop-loss settings are critical, and I believe the most important thing is for the trader to be consistent. Some traders set the stop-loss point based upon a Fibonacci ratio of the previous

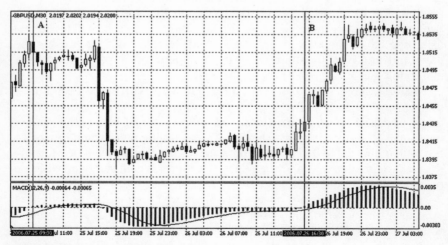

FIGURE 6.2   Crossovers July 25–26
Source: Copyright 2001–2007, MetaQuotes Software Corp.

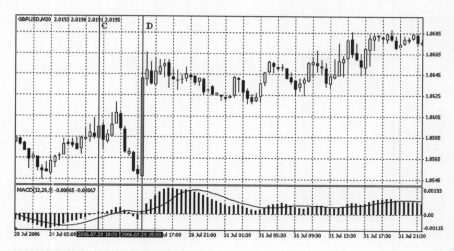

FIGURE 6.3 Crossovers July 28–31
Source: Copyright 2001–2007, MetaQuotes Software Corp.

move, while others use the previous support or resistance point plus a small margin of 10–15 pips. The stop-loss settings will not affect the overall outcome of our study. In any event, let's presume that the entry was made and the trade was not successful.

The next opportunity to reenter the market in the direction indicated by the day chart was presented at 16:30 the following day. The entry to the right of vertical line B would have been quite successful, and would offer the trader the ability to easily recover from the previous loss and to increase the trading account balance.

The next trading opportunity on July 28 at 10:30, as shown by vertical line C, in Figure 6.3, demonstrates how the market moved up about 15 pips and then retraced 40-plus pips before the large move in the direction of the overall trend. If the trader did not take the 10–15 pip profit, at that time, then he/she would have needed to wait for the completion of the retracement, which was not severe. The trade to the right of line D represents the most frightening entries because of the uncertainties of the placement of the stop-loss value. But, if the trader uses a default value of 40–50 pips, the overall outcome would be positive. As you can see, to the right of this entry the market eventually moved upward to provide the necessary profits.

Vertical line E, in Figure 6.4 shows, once again, a retracement before the real move upward. Once the trader has the confidence of the overall successes of the drill-down technique and of cost averaging, these retracements do not cause much stress.

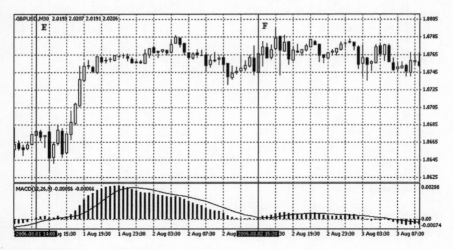

FIGURE 6.4 Crossovers August 1–2
Source: Copyright 2001–2007, MetaQuotes Software Corp.

The entry to the right of line F is more stressful for me as the market is range bound, and the longer it takes the more worrisome it becomes. The initial move up was about 20 pips, and the lowest point was negative 74 pips, before the significant move upward, as shown in Figure 6.4.

Figure 6.5 shows the entry up to the right of line F in greater detail. Once again, you can see that if the stop-loss value was reached and resulted in a losing trade, the next entry would have recovered from it. The entry to the right of line G, as you can see, would have been profitable.

In Figure 6.6, the entries up to the right of lines H and I offered 80 and 40 pips profit, respectively, with no need for cost averaging.

In the Figure 6.7 you can see the complete market movement following entry I upward as it set up for the losing entry to the right of line J. Entry J would be a loser by any standard. Whether a Fibonacci level or previous support or a fixed number of pips had been used, a loss would have developed. I displayed line I in this second picture for you to fully appreciate the complete movement and what was to follow. Once the stop-loss was reached to the right of line J, the market moved where it wanted to, causing us to wait for the next reason to reenter the market upward.

Figure 6.8 shows an example of a losing trade following another losing trade. As you may recall, the previous trade at line J did not make profit, and then we can see that the entry up to the right of line K would also not render profit. While the trade from line K was still open, I would not

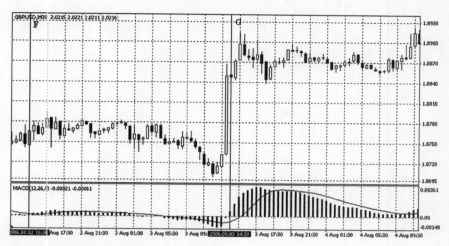

FIGURE 6.5 Crossovers August 2–3
Source: Copyright 2001–2007, MetaQuotes Software Corp.

consider entering to the right of lines L and M. The entry at line K would have included additional lots that would result in a greater loss, but this condition does not occur very often. An experienced trader would also point out that the MACD values were quite high indicating that the market was overbought.

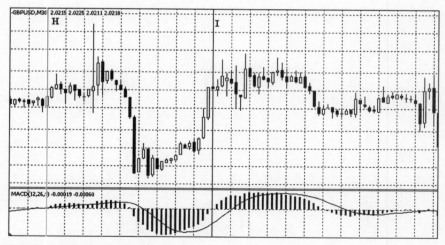

FIGURE 6.6 Crossovers August 5–8
Source: Copyright 2001–2007, MetaQuotes Software Corp.

FIGURE 6.7 Crossovers August 9–10
Source: Copyright 2001–2007, MetaQuotes Software Corp.

As you study the following trades, you will observe several trades that were not successful when the zero line was so high.

Again, I am showing an overlap in Figure 6.9 as you can see lines M, N, and O. The entry up to the right of line N would render the profits that we look for to recover the losses that were incurred in the previous two trades.

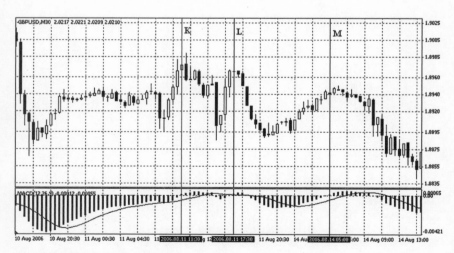

FIGURE 6.8 Crossovers August 11–14
Source: Copyright 2001–2007, MetaQuotes Software Corp.

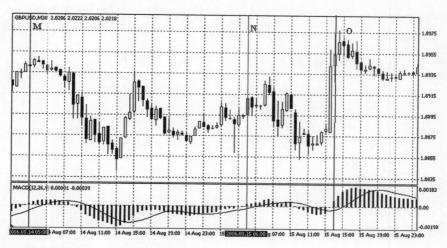

FIGURE 6.9 Crossovers August 14–15
Copyright 2001–2007, MetaQuotes Software Corp.

Notice how high the zero line is as we look for reasons to trade up. When the N trade opportunity develops, the zero line has returned to a mid-point position.

The entry up at line O (see Figure 6.10) would also not provide profits. This is the market condition that caused the day MACD to cross over to the down direction. When cost averaging, the trader should resist the

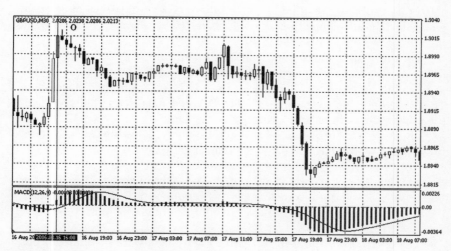

FIGURE 6.10 Crossovers August 16–17
Source: Copyright 2001–2007, MetaQuotes Software Corp.

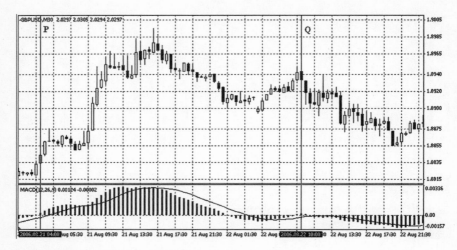

FIGURE 6.11 Crossovers August 20–22
Source: Copyright 2001–2007, MetaQuotes Software Corp.

temptation to attempt to recover too quickly, as we must always be prepared for the worst. In this case, there was one positive trade between two losers (if the trader entered at every vertical line regardless of the MACD zero line position).

The entry up to the right of line P, in Figure 6.11, resulted in a gain to offset the loss from the previous trade. I would recommend that this trade also consist of additional lots to speed the recovery. Trade Q, once again, places us in a losing position. We will need to view Figure 6.12 to evaluate the recovery from this point.

The entry up to the right of R is, once again, another very positive trade as the market moves upward as indicated.

Trade S in Figure 6.13 rendered over 40 pips before the retracement. The trade entry up to the right of line T would have remained open until the high to the right of line V was reached.

The next two entries up, W and X in Figure 6.14, both worked wonderfully well. Isn't it great when a plan comes together?

Now that we are feeling very good about the previous trade, the Forex gives us another challenge. The entry to the right of line Y in Figure 6.15 failed when the large retracement was encountered. But, trade AA assisted in the recovery as the market moved up 30-plus pips before retracing downward.

The entry up to the right of AB in Figure 6.16 did not render profits before taking us to a losing position. But, once again, the system needs to be relied upon to methodically wait for the next opportunity.

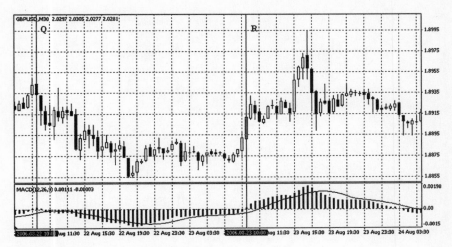

FIGURE 6.12 Crossovers August 22–23
Source: Copyright 2001–2007, MetaQuotes Software Corp.

The entry up to the right of line AC in Figure 6.17 would have lost, but notice how high the MACD zero line is.

In Figure 6.18, the bold line represents the MACD crossover on the day chart, so we now are looking for entries downward. The entry to the right of line AD paid over 50 pips before the retracement upward.

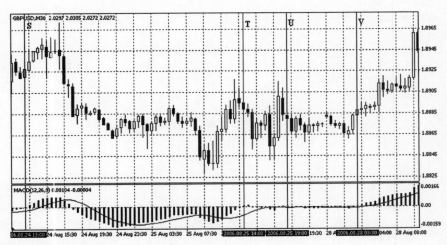

FIGURE 6.13 Crossovers August 24–28
Source: Copyright 2001–2007, MetaQuotes Software Corp.

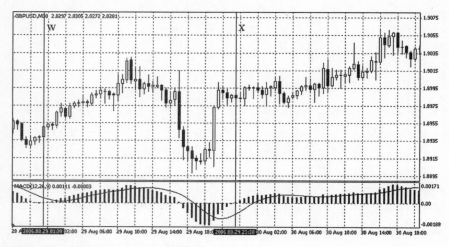

FIGURE 6.14 Crossovers August 29–30
Source: Copyright 2001–2007, MetaQuotes Software Corp.

The first entry down to the right of AF in Figure 6.19 did not work, so patience is called for as we wait for the next entry opportunity.

The entry down to the right of AG in Figure 6.20 worked well, while the entry down for AH rendered fewer than 30 pips before retracing upward.

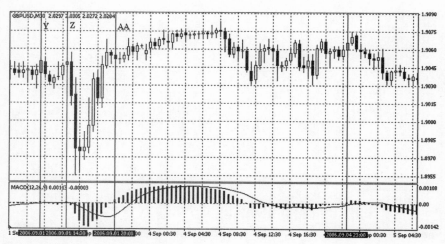

FIGURE 6.15 Crossovers September 1–4
Source: Copyright 2001–2007, MetaQuotes Software Corp.

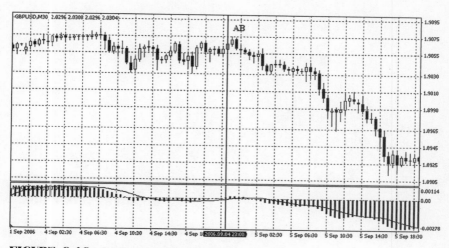

FIGURE 6.16 Crossovers September 4–5
Source: Copyright 2001–2007, MetaQuotes Software Corp.

The entries down to the right of lines AI and AJ in Figure 6.21 would be avoided if the trader was concerned about the relative position of the MACD zero line. On the right side of the chart, you can see the next bold vertical line indicating that the day chart MACD has crossed to the upward direction again.

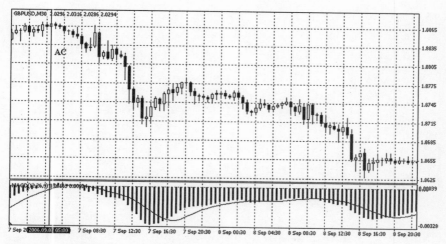

FIGURE 6.17 Crossovers September 7–8
Source: Copyright 2001–2007, MetaQuotes Software Corp.

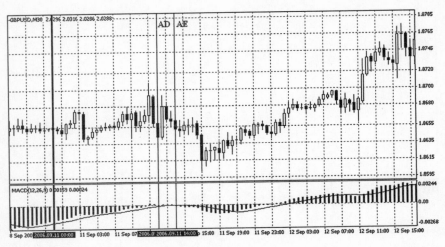

FIGURE 6.18 Crossovers September 8–12
Source: Copyright 2001–2007, MetaQuotes Software Corp.

The market was already in a lengthy move up, so it was four days before the first opportunity presented itself for a trade up. Figure 6.22 shows the entry up to the right of line AK that moved almost 50 pips before retracing back down.

The entry up to the right of line AL in Figure 6.23 was a losing trade. I must point out that, even though the MACD zero line is high, if the chart

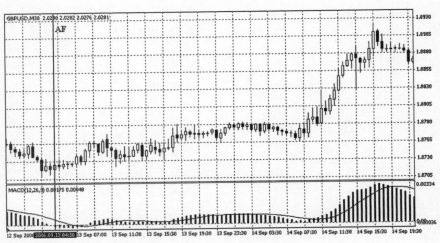

FIGURE 6.19 Crossovers September 12–14
Source: Copyright 2001–2007, MetaQuotes Software Corp.

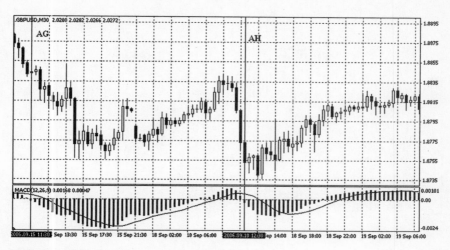

FIGURE 6.20 Crossovers September 15–18
Source: Copyright 2001–2007, MetaQuotes Software Corp.

positions that candle to the rightmost position, it is in the midpoint area; so I believe that a losing trade would have been entered at that point.

The market retraced to the right of line AM, but it did not reach below the previous support point. The trade would carry additional lots, and the stop-loss was a little large, but the results were positive. If the trader is

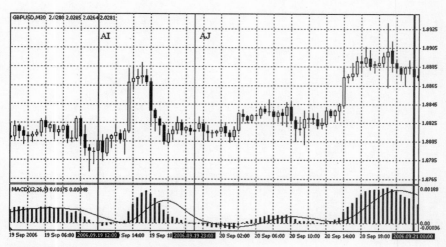

FIGURE 6.21 Crossovers September 19–20
Source: Copyright 2001–2007, MetaQuotes Software Corp.

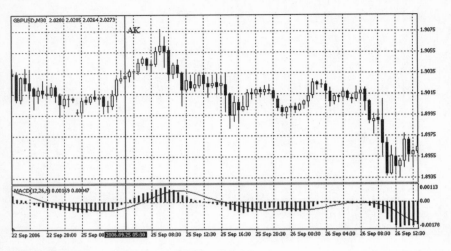

FIGURE 6.22 Crossovers September 22–26
Source: Copyright 2001–2007, MetaQuotes Software Corp.

uncomfortable with the stop-loss position, he/she should wait for the next trading opportunity. The market move up to the right of line AN was very positive and had a smaller stop-loss value (see Figure 6.24).

The trade entry up to the right of vertical line AO did not render profit before the new vertical line was drawn in bold from the day

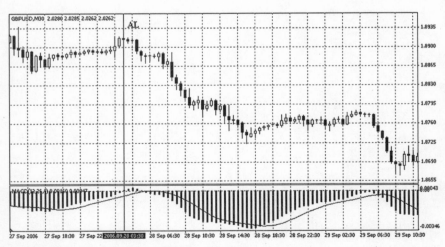

FIGURE 6.23 Crossovers September 27–29
Source: Copyright 2001–2007, MetaQuotes Software Corp.

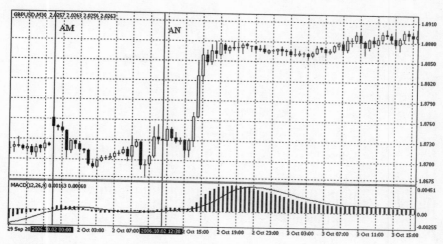

FIGURE 6.24 Crossovers September 29-Oct 3
Source: Copyright 2001–2007, MetaQuotes Software Corp.

chart. The day chart MACD crossed down at that point, so the trader would need to make a decision regarding the open trade going up. Notice the movement downward to the right of line AP (see Figure 6.25 and Figure 6.26).

The entry up to the right of vertical line AQ moved down nicely.

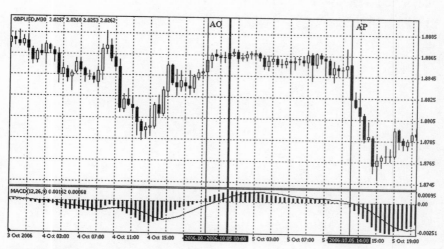

FIGURE 6.25 Crossovers October 4–5
Source: Copyright 2001–2007, MetaQuotes Software Corp.

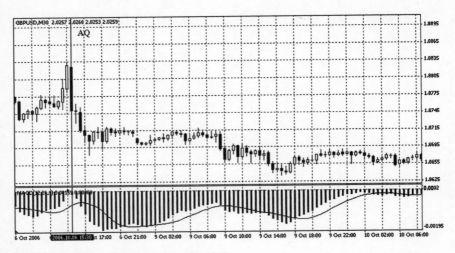

FIGURE 6.26 Crossovers October 6–9
Source: Copyright 2001–2007, MetaQuotes Software Corp.

SUMMARY

The above examples have purposely included some questionable trades
that turned bad in order to demonstrate the usefulness of the cost averaging technique. I am not an expert in the use of the MACD, and did not
elaborate on the regular and hidden divergence issues, but I was still able
to utilize this technique with positive results.

CHAPTER 7

Loss Recovery with Stochastics

The figures in this chapter will be limited to trading the Slow Stochastics crossovers only as shown for the GBP/USD currency combination. The settings on these examples are 12, 26 and 9. Only the crossovers will be employed for this study. Figure 7.1 shows bold vertical lines where the crossovers occurred on the day chart during the summer of 2006. We will examine four of these crossovers that began in May and extended into October. In Chapter 5, I discussed the "drill-down" technique using the day chart and the two-hour chart. In this study I am using the day chart and the 30-minute chart to demonstrate the versatility of the methodology.

These examples were chosen carefully to work with market conditions that are typical and not the best for trading. To the right of vertical lines 1 and 2, the market did go down and up, respectively, as expected. To the right of line 3, the market was flat while the oscillator was indicating downward movement. To the right of line 4, the market went down while the oscillator was pointing up. So, we have some good illustrations on how to look for cost average trading opportunities using the Slow Stochastics oscillator.

The first crossover down on the day chart was on May 19, and the first crossover down on the 30-minute chart occurred during the 5th hour as shown by line A in Figure 7.2. The entry to the right of line A would have rendered profits as the market followed the oscillator. The next entry to the right of line B would have been approximately 1.8716 and offered about 10 pips profit before retracing. The market had already moved 300 pips, so a retracement should be expected, and the profit potential should be

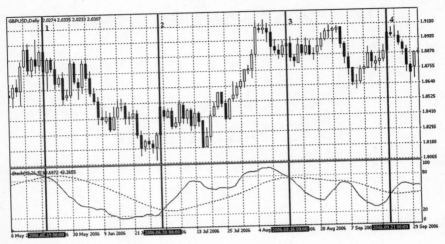

FIGURE 7.1 Day Chart Crossovers
Source: Copyright 2001–2007, MetaQuotes Software Corp.

lowered. This is a similar condition to what we saw in the previous chapter, where the previous supports and resistances are 50–80 pips away.

When trading on these larger time compressions, the stop-loss values will need to be more generous. This also means that it is discomforting to trade for 10–15 pips profit while providing for such large losses. The missing factor is the success rate of the trade. When the success rate is high, then the ratio is affected in a positive manner.

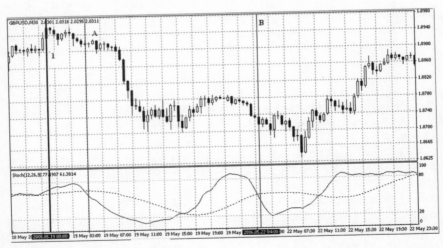

FIGURE 7.2 Crossovers May 18–22
Source: Copyright 2001–2007, MetaQuotes Software Corp.

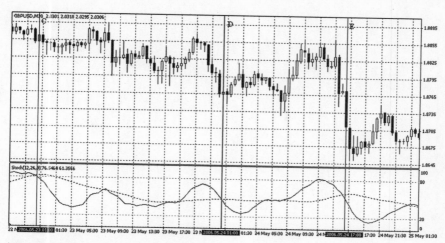

FIGURE 7.3 Crossovers May 22–24
Source: Copyright 2001–2007, MetaQuotes Software Corp.

The next trading opportunity on May 23 at 01:00, as shown by vertical line C in Figure 7.3, took time to develop, but it ultimately resulted in the expected profit. The trade down to the right of line D also performed well as it dropped approximately 30 pips before the retracement. The trade entry down to the right of line E also rendered 30-plus pips quickly.

Vertical lines F, G, and H in Figure 7.4 all show profits downward with little hesitation. You can see how well these typically work, but there will be challenges ahead.

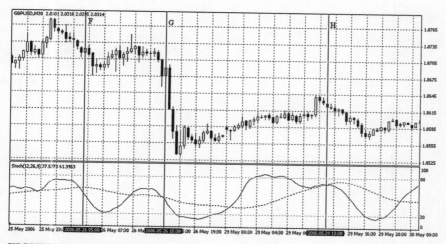

FIGURE 7.4 Crossovers May 25–29
Source: Copyright 2001–2007, MetaQuotes Software Corp.

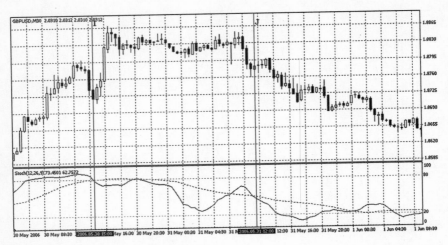

FIGURE 7.5 Crossovers May 30–31
Source: Copyright 2001–2007, MetaQuotes Software Corp.

Figure 7.5 shows our first loss to the right of line I. The market did look like it was going to retrace further, but it did not. So, we suffered the loss. The next entry down to the right of line J, however, provides us with an opportunity to trade with additional lots and to expect for more of a retracement.

The entry down to the right of line K in Figure 7.6 demonstrates another losing trade that had a small loss of less than 40 pips. The next

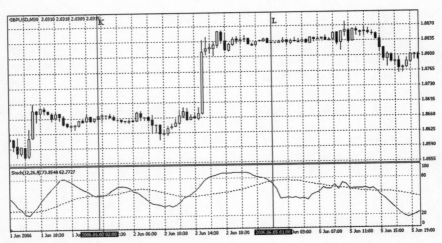

FIGURE 7.6 Crossovers June 1–2
Source: Copyright 2001–2007, MetaQuotes Software Corp.

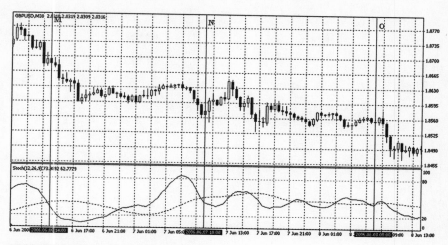

FIGURE 7.7 Crossovers June 6–7
Source: Copyright 2001–2007, MetaQuotes Software Corp.

trading opportunity down at line L shows the recovery as the market moves downward following the next entry.

The three trades shown in Figure 7.7 all moved down as indicated. This is what I look for when cost averaging.

It is difficult to determine the stop-loss value to use for the next trade down to the right of line P in Figure 7.8. The previous 30 candles were in a limited range, but they followed the large move down. I would use the range plus 15 or more pips. The range high was 1.8453, and the high to the right of line P was 1.8461.

The trade entry down at line Q is more problematic as it is late Friday afternoon when the market is closing. I would not enter this trade because of the uncertainties that weekends can bring. I would wait for the next cycle to enter.

The three trades in Figure 7.9 are all healthy and the retracements are consistent with the previous ranges. The trade down to the right of line R moved over 40 pips downward before retracing. The other two suffered retracements prior to achieving profits.

The entry down at line U (see Figure 7.10) occurred when an announcement was made. The gap would scare me into avoidance of this trade, if nothing else. Trading during announcements is extremely risky, and it is generally to be avoided. Some traders also avoid having any open positions when an economic announcement is imminent. I am not fearful of that, and I believe that the market uses announcements to fulfill the predictions revealed by technical indicators. So, avoiding open positions during

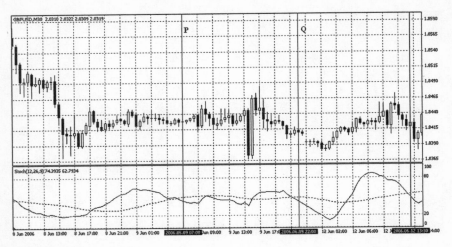

FIGURE 7.8 Crossovers June 8–9
Source: Copyright 2001–2007, MetaQuotes Software Corp.

announcements quite often results in lower profits. In this case, however, there are clear indications giving us pause.

The trade entry down to the right of line V is the one that I would have made, and it did not prove profitable. The trade entry to the right of line W would be profitable because of the large stop-loss value that it required. It

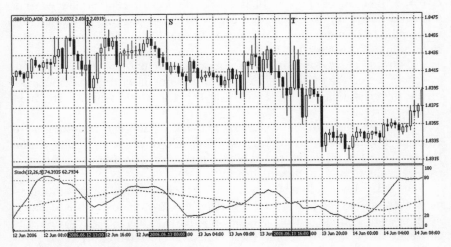

FIGURE 7.9 Crossovers June 12–13
Source: Copyright 2001–2007, MetaQuotes Software Corp.

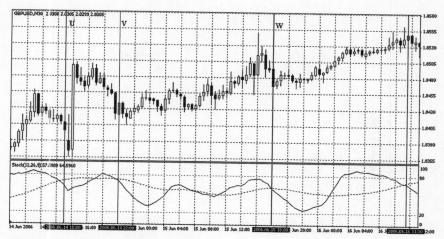

FIGURE 7.10 Crossovers June 14–15
Source: Copyright 2001–2007, MetaQuotes Software Corp.

would not have been profitable until the next line is reached, however. But, the trade at line W would have been with additional lots.

The entry down to the right of line X in Figure 7.11 with extra lots pays profits readily. The entry to the right of line Y is less eager.

The four entries down shown on Figure 7.12 were all very profitable as hoped for, except for AA, which retraced to 1.8467 before falling to the

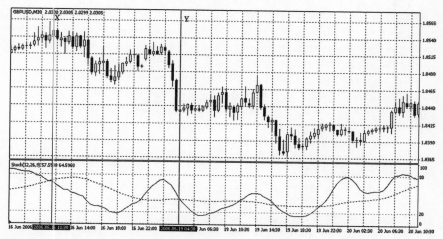

FIGURE 7.11 Crossovers June 16–19
Source: Copyright 2001–2007, MetaQuotes Software Corp.

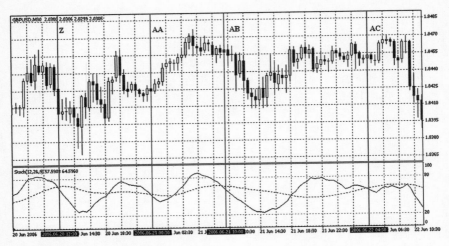

FIGURE 7.12 Crossovers June 20–21
Source: Copyright 2001–2007, MetaQuotes Software Corp.

desired level. The resistance level to the left of AA is 1.8451, so the market went just 16 pips higher.

This is a good illustration of the need for the trader to be generous with the stop-loss values. Please keep in mind that the true safety in these trades is in the selection of the direction of the trend as determined by the same oscillator on the day chart.

Trades AD and AE down paid fairly well, but AF rendered about 25 pips before retracing (see Figure 7.13).

The first two trades down on Figure 7.14 were easy, while trade AI retraced first and the correct procedure for setting the stop-loss value would have been adequate.

We are finally at the end of the downward trend as indicated by the day chart (see Figure 7.1). The trade to the right of AJ paid over 70 pips prior to the announcement where the large bullish candles appear. The bold vertical line is where the day chart oscillator crossed upward.

During the last downward section, the market behaved rather well. During the next one it was more erratic, so I expect to see more challenges (see Figure 7.15).

The entry up to the right of AK in Figure 7.16 moved up quickly to give us the desired profits. The first trading opportunity came 15 hours following the cross of the oscillator on the day chart.

The entry up to the right of line AL in Figure 7.17 might have lost, except that the market was moving downward so fast following the 14:00 announcement I would have hesitated to enter. The entry up to the right

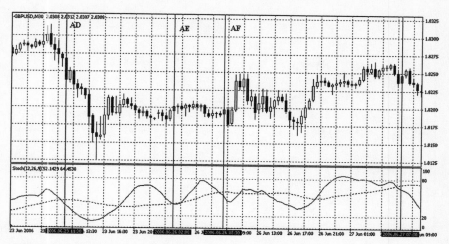

FIGURE 7.13 Crossovers June 23-26
Source: Copyright 2001-2007, MetaQuotes Software Corp.

of line AM immediately retraced after showing only 10 pips profit, but then fell over 100 pips to confirm that a loss would have occurred at this point.

In Figure 7.18, I am showing the AM trade again for clarity. The next trades demonstrate how the cost-averaged entry with extra lots following the bad one would have paid nicely.

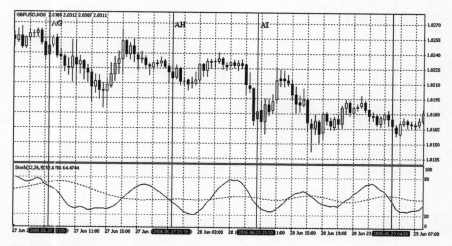

FIGURE 7.14 Crossovers June 27-28
Source: Copyright 2001-2007, MetaQuotes Software Corp.

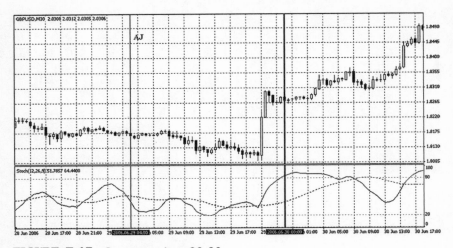

FIGURE 7.15   Crossovers June 28–29
Source: Copyright 2001–2007, MetaQuotes Software Corp.

The entry up to the right of AQ did not develop until the move upward following line AR. The entry up to the right of line AS moved upward about 25 pips prior to the retracement, and the entry at AT moved similarly (see Figure 7.19).

The entry up to the right of line AU worked well, while the AV entry did not. But, once again, the entry following the bad one did well in the

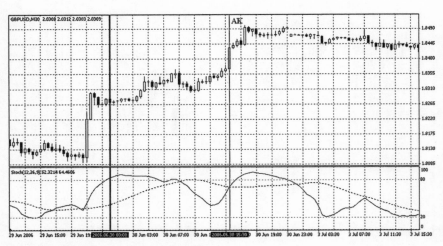

FIGURE 7.16   Crossovers June 29–30
Source: Copyright 2001–2007, MetaQuotes Software Corp.

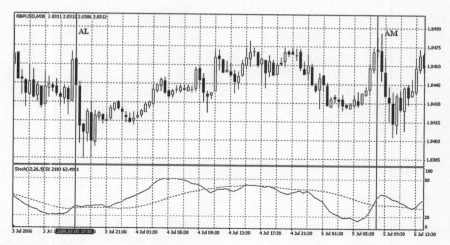

FIGURE 7.17 Crossovers July 3-4
Source: Copyright 2001-2007, MetaQuotes Software Corp.

direction of the overall trend. We are near the end of this retracement section on the day chart with minimal damage to our trades (see Figure 7.20).

The entries up to the right of line AX did not pay, while the next one paid about 30 pips before retracing. The Trade AZ also did not perform (see Figure 7.21).

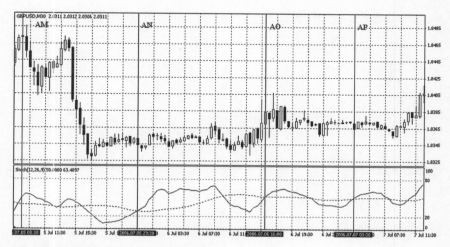

FIGURE 7.18 Crossovers July 5-6
Source: Copyright 2001-2007, MetaQuotes Software Corp.

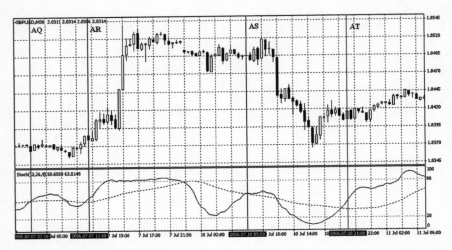

FIGURE 7.19 Crossovers July 7–10
Source: Copyright 2001–2007, MetaQuotes Software Corp.

The market gave healthy profits to the right of both lines BA and BB as the upward direction of the day chart Stochastic oscillator proved to be accurate (see Figure 7.22).

The entries up to the right of lines BC, BD, and BE all paid nicely (see Figure 7.23).

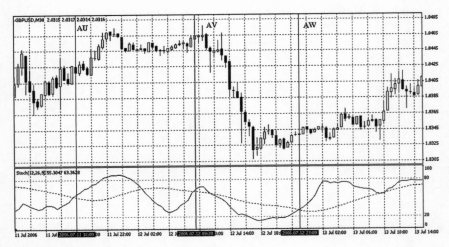

FIGURE 7.20 Crossovers July 11–12
Source: Copyright 2001–2007, MetaQuotes Software Corp.

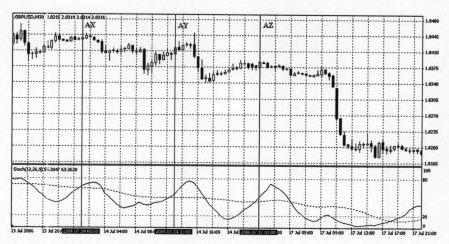

FIGURE 7.21 Crossovers July 13–17
Source: Copyright 2001–2007, MetaQuotes Software Corp.

The entry up to the right of line BF saw about 40 pips profit before the retracement, while the entry at BG failed to give any profits, given the large retracement. BH also saw about 30 pips before the retracement.

These trade entries up following the previous lackluster ones are very powerful. This is quite typical to see strong performance in agreement

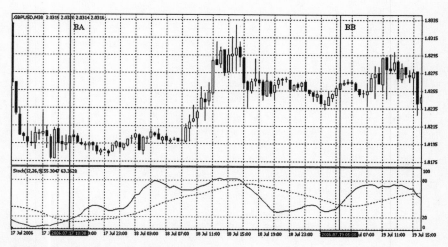

FIGURE 7.22 Crossovers July 17–18
Source: Copyright 2001–2007, MetaQuotes Software Corp.

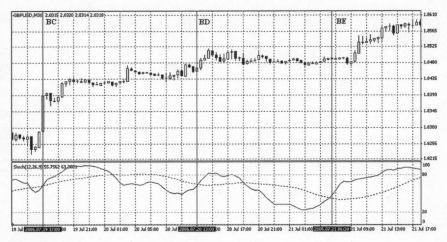

FIGURE 7.23 Crossovers July 19–20
Source: Copyright 2001–2007, MetaQuotes Software Corp.

with the day chart trend following a strong retracement as shown in
Figure 7.24.

The entry up to the right of vertical line BL paid directly, while the
next one basically waited for the market to move right of line BN (see
Figure 7.26).

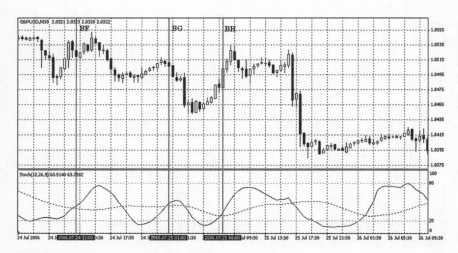

FIGURE 7.24 Crossovers July 24–25
Source: Copyright 2001–2007, MetaQuotes Software Corp.

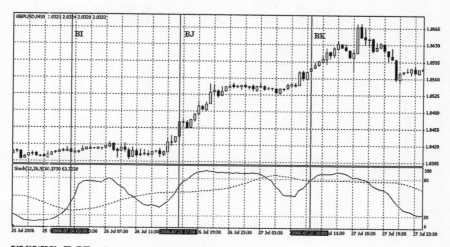

FIGURE 7.25 Crossovers July 25–27
Source: Copyright 2001–2007, MetaQuotes Software Corp.

The entries up on Figure 7.27 are both positive following the overall trend established by the day chart oscillator.

The entries up in Figure 7.25 to the right of lines BI, BJ, and BK, all performed as expected.

You can easily see that the trade entries up to the right of the vertical lines on Figure 7.28 both paid nicely.

The first trade entry is always uncertain in my mind when entering after a large move caused by an economic announcement. The second trade

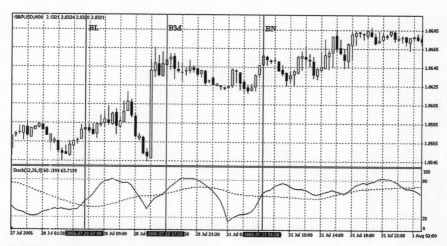

FIGURE 7.26 Crossovers July 27–31
Source: Copyright 2001–2007, MetaQuotes Software Corp.

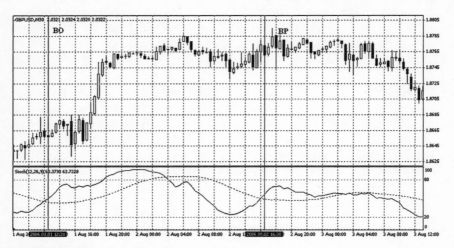

FIGURE 7.27 Crossovers August 1-2
Source: Copyright 2001-2007, MetaQuotes Software Corp.

entry is still uncertain as I look back and wonder if a 50 percent retracement is about to develop. Trusting the technical signal is always a challenge for the trader.

All three entries up represented in Figure 7.29 were successful. Notice how the trades tend to move upward better when the oscillator is in a lower position.

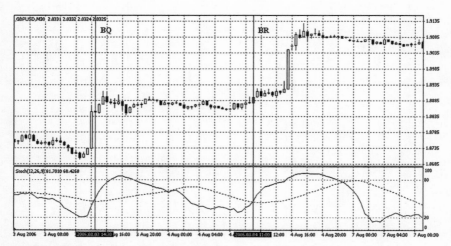

FIGURE 7.28 Crossovers August 3-4
Source: Copyright 2001-2007, MetaQuotes Software Corp.

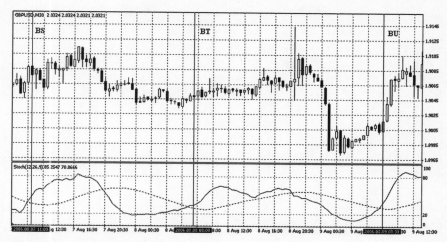

FIGURE 7.29 Crossovers August 7–8
Source: Copyright 2001–2007, MetaQuotes Software Corp.

The trade entry up on Figure 7.30 to the right of BV only paid about 25 pips before retracing. The trade entry to the right of BW rendered over 50 pips before its retracement, but the BX trade gave only about 20 pips profit.

Because we cannot predict the exact movement before it occurs, we must always be prepared for a general move of 20–30 pips.

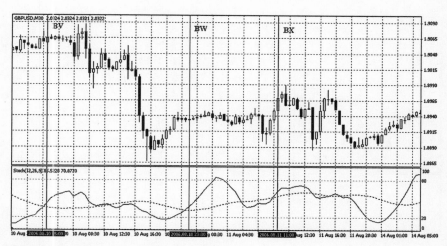

FIGURE 7.30 Crossovers August 10–11
Source: Copyright 2001–2007, MetaQuotes Software Corp.

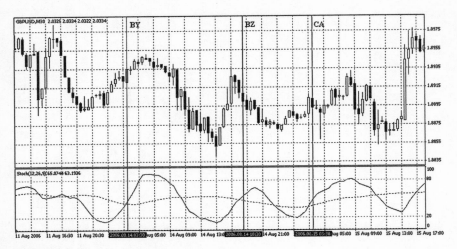

FIGURE 7.31 Crossovers August 11–14
Source: Copyright 2001–2007, MetaQuotes Software Corp.

The trade entry up to the right of line BY provided only about 10 pips profit before making a 90-plus pip retracement. The following trade at line BZ would have been the recovery using the cost average technique with additional lots. The trade at line CA also performed well (see Figure 7.31).

The trade entry up to the right of line CB, as shown in Figure 7.32, is the last in this series of up trades as indicated by the oscillator on the day chart.

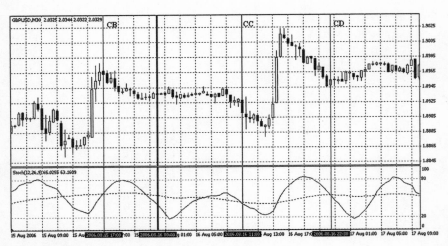

FIGURE 7.32 Crossovers August 15–16
Source: Copyright 2001–2007, MetaQuotes Software Corp.

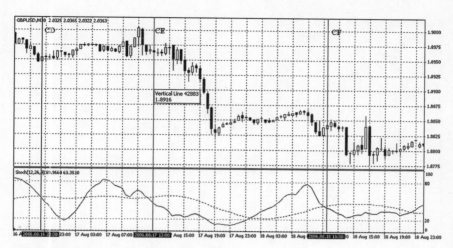

FIGURE 7.33 Crossovers August 16–17
Source: Copyright 2001–2007, MetaQuotes Software Corp.

This trade did not make profit until the following trade had cleared, and would present the trader with an interesting decision at the point of the CC entry. The CC entry itself only rendered about 25 pips profit, so the trader could have left the original stop-value in place, or could have closed the CB trade with a loss and added more lots to the CC trade. The CD trade entry down paid very well, as will be shown in the next figure.

The trade entry CD in Figure 7.33 lingered before paying to the right of line CE, which performed very well. The entry down to the right of line CF also did well.

So far in this chapter, we have experienced fairly consistent successful trade entries. In each case where a loss occurred, we were able to make up for it in the next trade that was presented.

Both of the trade entry points down in Figure 7.34 show easy profits with no stress.

Both of the trade entries down in Figure 7.35 also paid fairly quickly with little retracement.

For the past several trades, the market behaved almost too well. Now we are faced with a couple of challenges as shown in Figure 7.36.

The two trades down—CK and CL—did not render profits as the market did not follow the oscillator. The trade entry CK would have hit my stop-loss value, as would have CL. When this happens, I do not abandon the system that I follow, but I continue to forge ahead with persistency. The trade entry to the right of CM would start the recovery process as I would trade once again with additional lots.

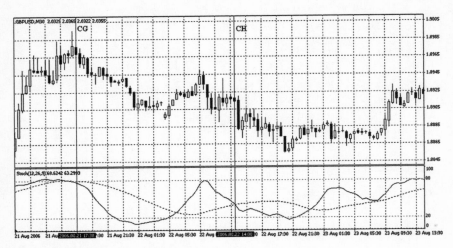

FIGURE 7.34 Crossovers August 21–22
Source: Copyright 2001–2007, MetaQuotes Software Corp.

Figure 7.37 shows four potential trade entries down, the first of which worked well. The entry to the right of line CO did not, however, and the oscillation for entry CP was very weak. I believe that I would have traded each of these only because the stop-loss values were fairly small. You might feel like you are being pecked to death, but the risk reward ratio is too compelling to not try.

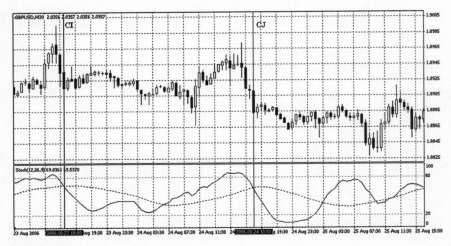

FIGURE 7.35 Crossovers August 23–24
Source: Copyright 2001–2007, MetaQuotes Software Corp.

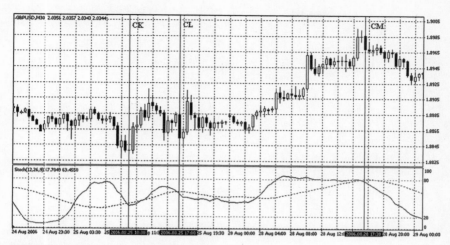

FIGURE 7.36 Crossovers August 24-25
Source: Copyright 2001-2007, MetaQuotes Software Corp.

Persistency in this business usually is worth it as you can see with the action in Figure 7.38, where all three trade entries performed as expected and without much delay. Here is where we are able to recover from the previous losses. When suffering two or more losses in sequence, I do not attempt to recover everything with one trade, but spread it out over the next three or four entries.

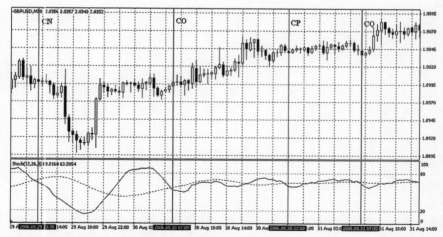

FIGURE 7.37 Crossovers August 29-30
Source: Copyright 2001-2007, MetaQuotes Software Corp.

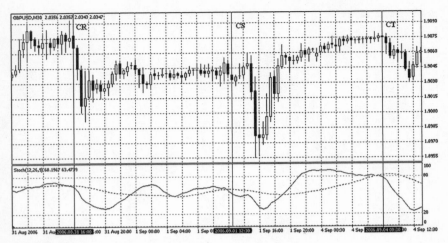

FIGURE 7.38 Crossovers August 31-September 1
Source: Copyright 2001–2007, MetaQuotes Software Corp.

Figure 7.39 also contains good trade entries down that resulted in substantial profits for the trader. When the market goes against the day chart oscillator, as shown in Figure 7.37, I always expect to see a fairly substantial recovery, which is what we see here.

The trade entries down shown in Figure 7.40 also did well, which continues our streak of successes.

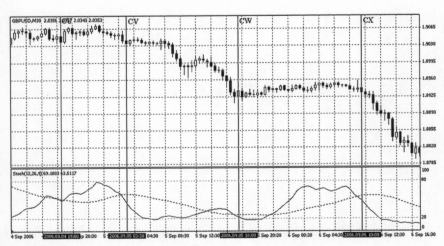

FIGURE 7.39 Crossovers September 4–5
Source: Copyright 2001–2007, MetaQuotes Software Corp.

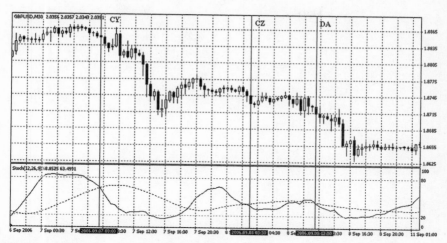

FIGURE 7.40 Crossovers September 6–7
Source: Copyright 2001–2007, MetaQuotes Software Corp.

The entry down to the right of line DB in Figure 7.41 paid well, but the next one suffered a loss. The loss was not large, as the stop-loss value was relatively small. The entry DD, however, offered the recovery in short order.

As shown by this study of the use of the Slow Stochastics, there are seldom multiple losses in a row. But, here we are faced with two beginning

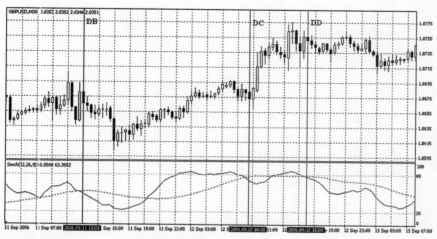

FIGURE 7.41 Crossovers September 11–12
Source: Copyright 2001–2007, MetaQuotes Software Corp.

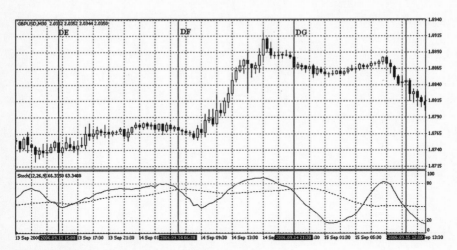

FIGURE 7.42 Crossovers September 13–14
Source: Copyright 2001–2007, MetaQuotes Software Corp.

with the entry down to the right of lines DE and DF. The DF entry offered about 10 pips profit before retracing, but the stop-loss value would have been small. The DG trade starts the recovery process (see Figure 7.42).

The first two entries down shown in Figure 7.43 worked well, but the final entry DJ does not show the eventual run upward resulting in a loss.

Figure 7.44 shows one last entry down before the day chart oscillator changed to the upward direction. The trade entry previous to the DK entry

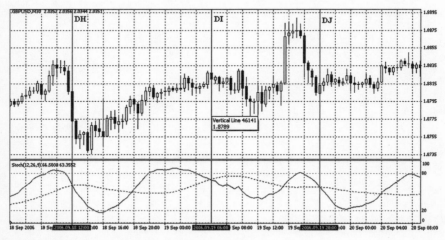

FIGURE 7.43 Crossovers September 18–19
Source: Copyright 2001–2007, MetaQuotes Software Corp.

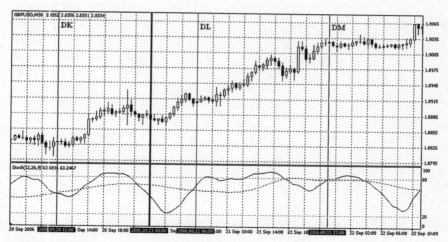

FIGURE 7.44 Crossovers September 20–21
Source: Copyright 2001–2007, MetaQuotes Software Corp.

suffered a loss, and the DK entry also did not perform, but the stop-loss value would have been relatively small. The entries to the right of lines DL and DM would provide the recovery for those other losses.

If you look at Figure 7.1 you will see that the market did not move in the direction of the oscillator on the day chart to the right of line 4. Figure 7.44 shows gains made before the large move down.

Figure 7.45 allows the trader to earn profits at entry DN, but the entry up to the right of DO would have retraced immediately. Line DP provides the trader with an automatic cost average entry that should be taken advantage of. The DP entry offered the chance for recovery.

Here come the challenges as the market moves down while giving weak signals for the trader who wants to trade up.

The entry up to the right of line DQ is given no chance for profit. Entries DR and DS are basically the same, so I would not enter again to the right of DS. The losses for the DQ, DR, and DT entries would be minimal as the stop-loss values would be small.

We are now in the midst of the horrible looking retracement on the day chart (see Figure 7.46).

Figure 7.47 shows an ugly picture as the two entries up offer less than 30 pips each. This is where my expectations would be fairly high as we have already seen the market go against the day chart.

I am purposely including this in my study for you to see and understand better how to deal with this situation. In these two entries, I might have taken two losses in an attempt to obtain greater gains as expected.

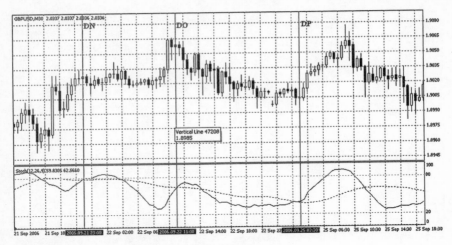

FIGURE 7.45 Crossovers September 21-22
Source: Copyright 2001-2007, MetaQuotes Software Corp.

But, I do not trade a large percentage of the account, and I do not become discouraged.

Figure 4.48 concludes our study of the Slow Stochastic oscillator for cost averaging purposes. As you can see, the entries up represented by lines DW–DY assisted in the recovery from the previous losses. This just reinforces the importance of consistency.

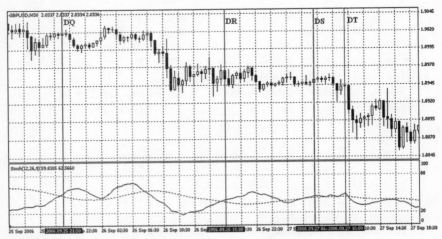

FIGURE 7.46 Crossovers September 25-26
Source: Copyright 2001-2007, MetaQuotes Software Corp.

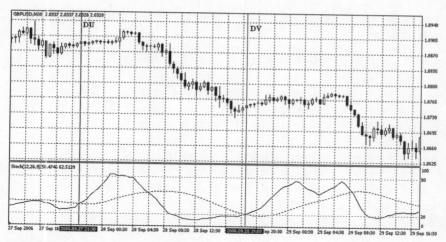

FIGURE 7.47 Crossovers September 27–28
Source: Copyright 2001–2007, MetaQuotes Software Corp.

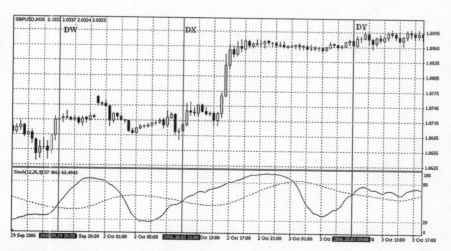

FIGURE 7.48 Crossovers September 29-Oct 2
Source: Copyright 2001–2007, MetaQuotes Software Corp.

SUMMARY

This study included the various conditions that are presented to the trader by the Forex market. The dynamics are sometimes difficult to interpret, but the trader following a technical system is able to be persistent and is, therefore, able to take advantage of the recoveries that generally occur with regularity.

The above examples have purposely included some questionable trades that turned bad in order to demonstrate the usefulness of the cost averaging technique. I think that the Slow Stochastic oscillator is more effective than the MACD that was studied in Chapter 6. There are many traders who rely on this oscillator for initial trade entries, while this study used it for second entries. This study presumed that a trader was already in the market with a trade going badly. These entries could be used to cost average or to hedge the initial entry.

The next three chapters describe what I feel are progressively better tools for use while trading the Forex. If your eyes are glazing over with all of this detail, I suggest that you don't give up, but continue to follow my lead and pick up some important "million dollar" tips.

CHAPTER 8

Loss Recovery with Moving Averages

T he figures in this chapter will be limited to trading the moving average crossovers only as shown for the GBP/USD currency combination. The settings on these examples are 5 and 20 candles based on the closing values using the simple method. Only the crossovers will be employed for this study. Figure 8.1 shows bold vertical lines where the crossovers occurred on the day chart during the summer of 2006. We will examine eight of these crossovers that began in May and extended into October. In Chapter 5, I discussed the drill-down technique using the day chart and the two-hour chart. In this study I am using the day chart and the 30-minute chart to demonstrate the versatility of the methodology. If you compare Figure 8.1 with Figure 7.1, you will notice how these settings result in an earlier crossover for line 2, but fewer crossovers to the right of line 2. You can use this to your advantage when looking for a reason to enter a trade as a way to cost average an already open position. If one technical indicator is not in position to enter a trade, then maybe another one will be. So, it might be necessary to search for the best opportunity among these various options.

These examples were chosen carefully to work with market conditions that are typical and not the best for trading.

To the right of vertical line 1 in Figure 8.1 the market did go down as predicted by the oscillating lines. To the right of lines 2 and 3, the market did not perform as expected. Line 4 began a substantial move upward, and we will have many good trading opportunities in this period. Lines 5 through 8 are very difficult, as you will see during this study. In spite of these difficulties, you will discover that these tools can be used to your

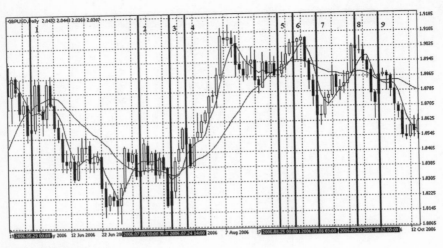

FIGURE 8.1   Day Chart
Source: Copyright 2001–2007, MetaQuotes Software Corp.

advantage. In any event, the entries should not be made using this one chart, but only after drilling-down to the 30-minute chart and waiting for 30-minute oscillation crossovers in the same direction.

The first crossover down on the day chart was on May 29, but the first crossover down on the 30-minute chart following was just a few hours later at 16:30, and it rendered profits almost immediately (see Figure 8.2).

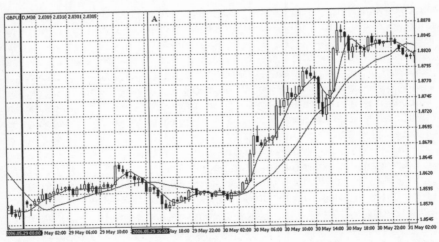

FIGURE 8.2   Crossovers May 29–30
Source: Copyright 2001–2007, MetaQuotes Software Corp.

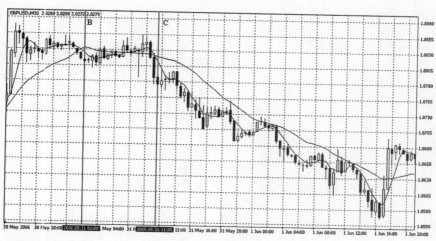

FIGURE 8.3 Crossovers May 30–June 1
Source: Copyright 2001–2007, MetaQuotes Software Corp.

The large move up was going the wrong direction, so no entries are shown. The stop-loss value for this entry would have needed to be above 1.8645, which is fairly large, but when trading on these larger time compressions the stops need to be larger.

The next crossover trading opportunity, as shown by vertical line B, gave about 25 pips on that quick spike down to its right and then went further after line C was formed. The crossover trade to the right of line C did very well (see Figure 8.3).

Vertical line D did not offer any profit until line E was formed, and then over 30 pips were offered before the retracement.

I must point out that I look for angle and separation of the moving average lines coming into the crossovers. This helps to avoid entries when the market is moving sideways. I will point them out as we continue this study.

Notice that the market conditions leading into lines D and E are not good. I would not have entered to the right of line D, and the candle to the left of line E is tempting, but line E itself is a doji, so I might have passed on that one also. I would prefer to see more separation between the moving average lines to the left of line E. Notice that there is white space between the moving average lines to the left of line F. The crossover entry to the right of line F paid quickly (see Figure 8.4).

Figure 8.5 includes four good crossover trades, except that lines I and J have no moving average separation. I would have passed on these two trade entries.

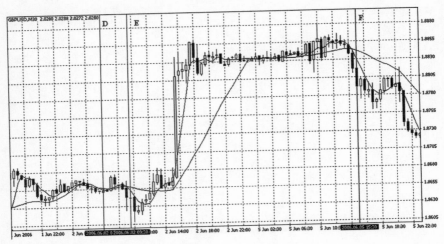

FIGURE 8.4 Crossovers June 1–5
Source: Copyright 2001–2007, MetaQuotes Software Corp.

Lines K, L, and M in Figure 8.6 demonstrate more entries to be avoided. Line M is also frightful because of the large move that was made. You never know when to get in and when not to on these large candles, so I usually do not try. We will examine the entry to the right of line O in the commentary for Figure 8.7.

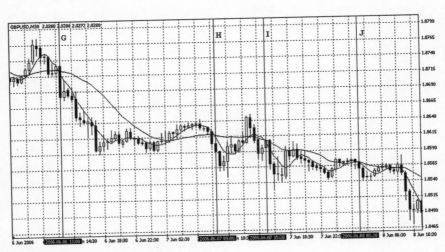

FIGURE 8.5 Crossovers June 6–7
Source: Copyright 2001–2007, MetaQuotes Software Corp.

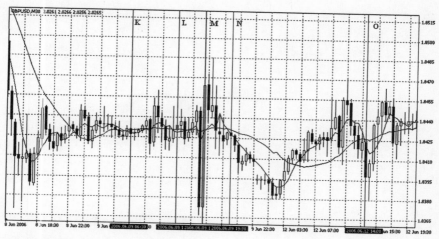

FIGURE 8.6 Crossovers June 8–12
Source: Copyright 2001–2007, MetaQuotes Software Corp.

The crossover trade entry down to the right of line O did pay good profits, but the market retraced first. It is usually stressful when entering to the right of a move like this because you never know when the market will retest the opposing resistance before making a commitment in the direction of your trade. The crossover entries down to the right of lines P and Q did quite well.

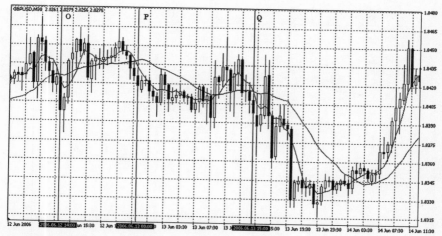

FIGURE 8.7 Crossovers June 12–13
Source: Copyright 2001–2007, MetaQuotes Software Corp.

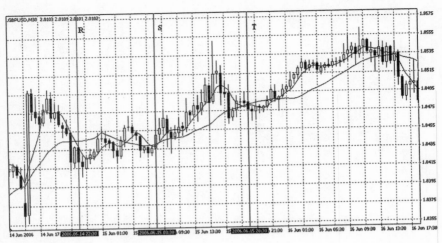

FIGURE 8.8 Crossovers June 14–16
Source: Copyright 2001–2007, MetaQuotes Software Corp.

The next crossover trade down to the right of line R did not pay before line S was formed, so the two trades are one and ended in a loss (see Figure 8.7). But, the crossover entry down to the right of line T paid very well, as is shown on Figure 8.8.

The four crossover trades down in Figure 8.9 are all healthy, and the retracements are consistent with the previous ranges. The trade to the right of line W moved over 40 pips downward before retracing.

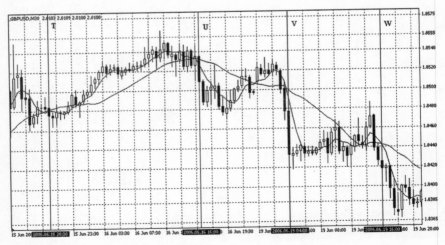

FIGURE 8.9 Crossovers June 16–19
Source: Copyright 2001–2007, MetaQuotes Software Corp.

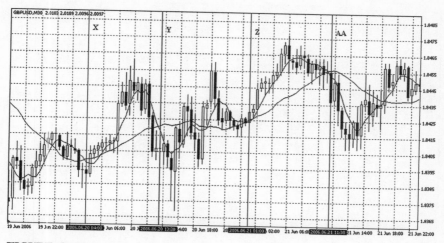

FIGURE 8.10 Crossovers June 19–21
Source: Copyright 2001–2007, MetaQuotes Software Corp.

The crossover entry down at line X (see Figure 8.10) performed poorly and the stop-loss value was hit ending in a loss. The entry down to the right of line Y did result in profits of about 30 pips, which I think is adequate for this type of trading, especially when adding extra lots after the losing trade. The entry down to the right of line Z immediately moved in the wrong direction, and when this happens, I usually will exit the trade as soon as I see the moving average crossing back up. When this happens, the next crossover trade offered will usually be more accommodating as you can see with line AA when the market exceeded the previous high to the left of the entry point.

The crossover entry down to the right of line AB as shown in Figure 8.11 should not be entered because the lines have no separation to the left. The same could be said for both entry points AC and AD.

One of the things that I look for in this situation is a breakout below the previous support point, especially if the support point is well defined, as it is in both of these examples. I would be comfortable entering below these support points knowing that the market has decided to move further in that direction. In this case, my profit expectations are lessened to maybe 10–15 pips per move.

The crossover entry down to the right of line AE in Figure 8.12 rendered about 20 pips before retracing. Entry AF is one of those that I would immediately exit out of fear that it would continue in the wrong direction. AG is a classic entry down to look for as the market retraces after the move upward. The crossover entry AH paid profits after a small retracement.

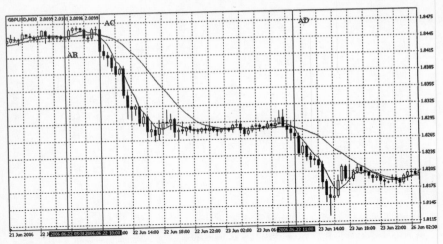

FIGURE 8.11 Crossovers June 21–23
Source: Copyright 2001–2007, MetaQuotes Software Corp.

Figure 8.13 shows only one vertical line, which is not a valid entry point because there is so little separation between the moving average lines to its left. When looking to trade down at this point, I would wait for a better opportunity.

The only crossover trade entry down on Figure 8.14 did very well, but the large move up might be intimidating.

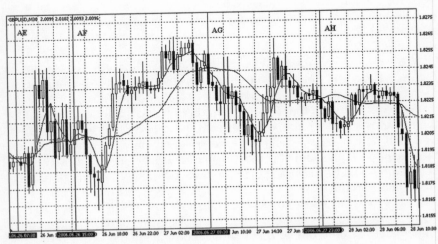

FIGURE 8.12 Crossovers June 26–27
Source: Copyright 2001–2007, MetaQuotes Software Corp.

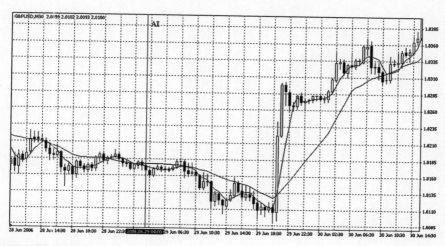

FIGURE 8.13 Crossovers June 28–29
Source: Copyright 2001–2007, MetaQuotes Software Corp.

We are finally at the end of the downward trend as indicated by the day chart (see Figure 8.1). The bold vertical line is where the day chart oscillator crossed upward. The entry to the right of line AK did not produce, nor did AL. The line AM finally produced to the right of line AO, and line AN had no separation to its left and would not merit an entry. The lines AK and

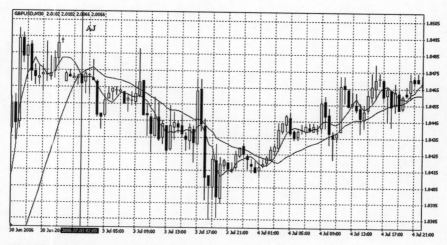

FIGURE 8.14 Crossovers June 30–July 4
Source: Copyright 2001–2007, MetaQuotes Software Corp.

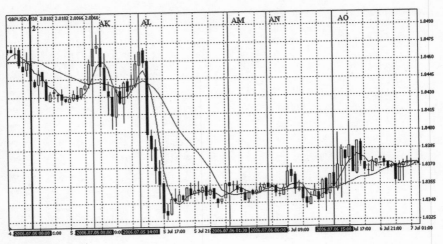

FIGURE 8.15 Crossovers July 4–6
Source: Copyright 2001–2007, MetaQuotes Software Corp.

AL would be very disappointing as the trader would expect to see better performance right after the day chart crossover occurred (see Figure 8.15). Once again this demonstrates the importance of trader persistence.

    The crossover entry up to the right of AP in Figure 8.16 moved up quickly to give us the desired profits. AQ also paid quickly. The entry up

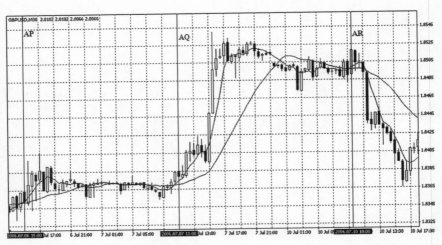

FIGURE 8.16 Crossovers July 6–10
Source: Copyright 2001–2007, MetaQuotes Software Corp.

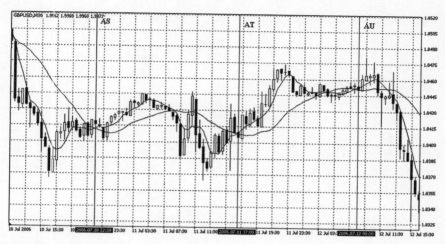

FIGURE 8.17 Crossovers July 10–11
Source: Copyright 2001–2007, MetaQuotes Software Corp.

to the right of line AR was a loser just when it looked like a great move upward would develop. All you can say to yourself is, "Welcome to the Forex."

The crossover entry up to the right of lines AS and AT on Figure 8.17 moved up as expected, and the AU entry moved up 30 pips before retracing.

In Figure 8.18, both of the entries paid 30 or more pips.

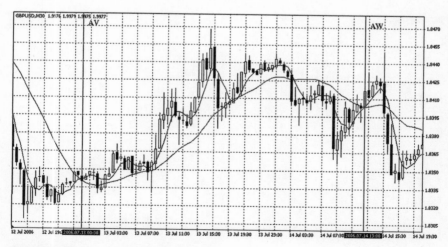

FIGURE 8.18 Crossovers July 12–14
Source: Copyright 2001–2007, MetaQuotes Software Corp.

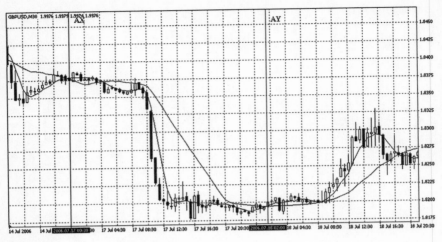

FIGURE 8.19 Crossovers July 14–18
Source: Copyright 2001–2007, MetaQuotes Software Corp.

The crossover entry up to the right of AX in Figure 8.19 did not develop, but the stop-loss value did its work, and the entry up to the right of line AY made the recovery.

The crossover entry down to the right of line AZ on Figure 8.20 reversed on the next candle, which is always a sign for me to kill the trade and wait for a better opportunity.

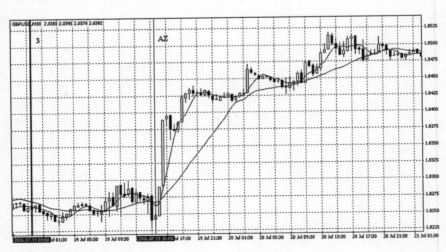

FIGURE 8.20 Crossovers July 19–20
Source: Copyright 2001–2007, MetaQuotes Software Corp.

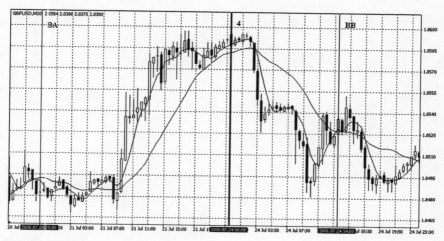

FIGURE 8.21 Crossovers July 21–24
Source: Copyright 2001–2007, MetaQuotes Software Corp.

If you look at the day chart on Figure 8.1, you will see that this is the small cross down where the moving average indicator was lagging and did not give an accurate reading of the market. Fortunately we can trade from this smaller time compression and bail out of a bad trade early. When my first candle, after entering a trade, moves badly like this one, I will exit and wait.

The crossover entry down to the right of line BA during this turbulent period did not render profits. Vertical line 4 represents the shift on the day chart to begin looking for trade entries up. Line BB is the first cross in that direction, and it also did not give profits.

But, let me point out that I look for space to the left of the vertical line and inside of the moving average lines. In Figure 8.21, I drew the vertical line too soon. I should wait one more candle in order to see that gap, and that would have resulted in a better entry price. This little white space is important. You will observe that I have tried to draw the vertical lines in this manner throughout this book.

The market moved against the trade immediately to the right of line BC in Figure 8.22 causing us to exit quickly. The crossover entry up to the right of line BD was not much better.

The last four entries have been difficult as the bankers move the market to recover their money. This tactic of exiting early when the market moves against a trade results in a great loss avoidance while we wait for the better market moves, as shown to the right of lines BE and BF.

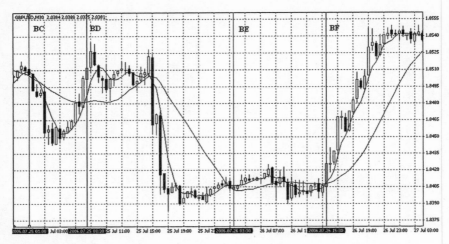

FIGURE 8.22 Crossovers July 25–26
Source: Copyright 2001–2007, MetaQuotes Software Corp.

The crossover entry up to the right of lines BG and BH in Figure 8.23 paid promptly, but BI required such a large stop-loss value that it would be best to wait.

The crossover entry up to the right of line BJ in Figure 8.24 paid very well after some hesitation. The BK entry also paid well.

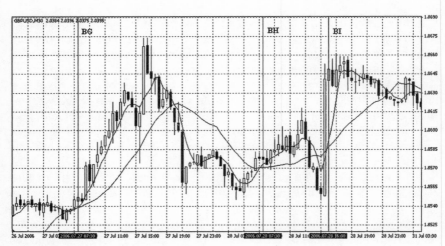

FIGURE 8.23 Crossovers July 26–28
Source: Copyright 2001–2007, MetaQuotes Software Corp.

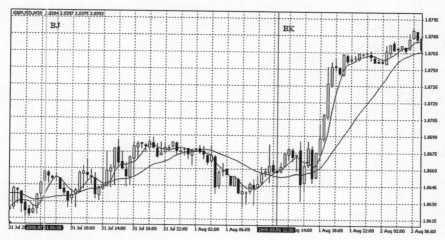

FIGURE 8.24 Crossovers July 31–August 1
Source: Copyright 2001–2007, MetaQuotes Software Corp.

The crossover trade entry up for line BL in Figure 8.25 did not perform until the market moved as shown by line BN. The market at the point of line BM was not moving, and I would wait for the next cross upward to be sure.

Figure 8.26 shows the crossover entries up to the right of vertical lines BP, BQ and BR paid right away. Yes!

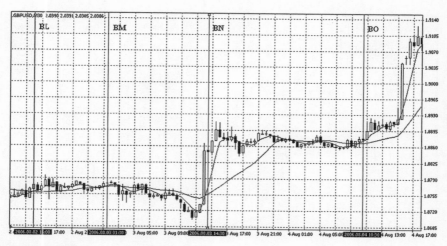

FIGURE 8.25 Crossovers August 2–4
Source: Copyright 2001–2007, MetaQuotes Software Corp.

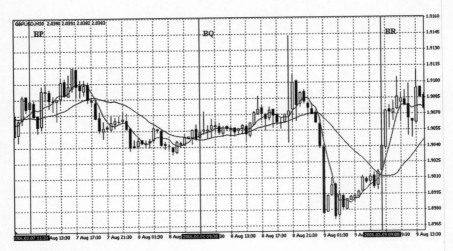

FIGURE 8.26 Crossovers August 7–8
Source: Copyright 2001–2007, MetaQuotes Software Corp.

The crossover entry up to the right of vertical lines BS (see Figure 8.27) paid only about 20 pips before retracing. The BT entry did much better. But, the BV entry never gave us a chance to make profit. I must admit that this move against the trade would be most difficult to manage because it was so much so fast. In any event, a loss would occur.

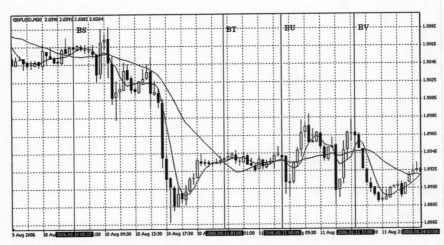

FIGURE 8.27 Crossovers August 9–11
Source: Copyright 2001–2007, MetaQuotes Software Corp.

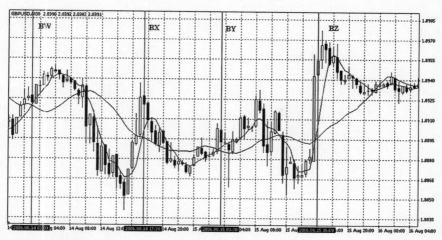

FIGURE 8.28 Crossovers August 14–15
Source: Copyright 2001–2007, MetaQuotes Software Corp.

Figure 8.28 shows four crossover entry opportunities upward. The BW entry move about 30 pips, which you have noticed by now is quite typical. The BX entry did not reach the stop-loss value, and it gave the trader a chance to enter a second cost average trade at line BY. Line BZ shows where the best entry could have been made.

The four crossover entries up represented in Figure 8.29 were mixed. The first worked well, while the second occurred during a flat market, and I would not have entered there. The entry at line CC eventually hit the very large stop-loss value, while CD rendered about 30 pips, where I would have been using extra lots as a cost average for the CC entry.

The crossover trade entry up in Figure 8.30 to the right of CD did not perform, but with additional lots, the entry at line CE would offer the desired recovery.

The crossover trade entry up to the right of line CI in Figure 8.31 provided about 25 pips before retracing. The entries for lines CG and CH did much better. The entry for CI did not perform depending upon how generous the stop-loss value was set, because the market did recover, as you will see in Figure 8.32.

The bold vertical line 5, as shown in Figure 8.32, represents the cross on the day chart to let us know that we should be looking for trades going down. The entry down to the right of line CJ would have paid nicely, while the CK entry would not. The whiplash at line CL is not a pretty sight, and would have resulted in a loss. The entry down at line CN is during a flat market, and I would not enter there.

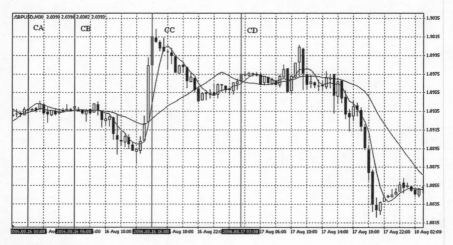

FIGURE 8.29 Crossovers August 16–17
Source: Copyright 2001–2007, MetaQuotes Software Corp.

Figure 8.33 shows two good crossover trades down followed by one that you know by now to exit immediately when the first candle reverses the direction of the trend.

Figure 8.34 shows the bold vertical line 6 where the day chart lines crossed up. So, we are now looking only for entries in that direction.

The crossover entry up to the right of line CR gave a maximum of about 15 pips before retracing, while the entry for line CS did not result in any

FIGURE 8.30 Crossovers August 17–21
Source: Copyright 2001–2007, MetaQuotes Software Corp.

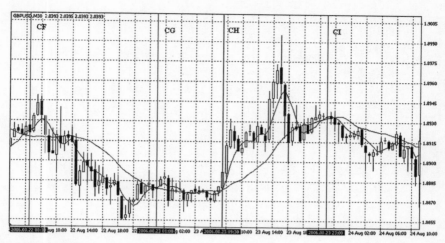

FIGURE 8.31 Crossovers August 22-23
Source: Copyright 2001–2007, MetaQuotes Software Corp.

profit. The CT entry point is too flat, but the CU entry resulted in about 30 pips profit.

These are difficult entries that did not perform as well. By now you might have observed the noticeable turbulence caused when the day chart moving lines cross.

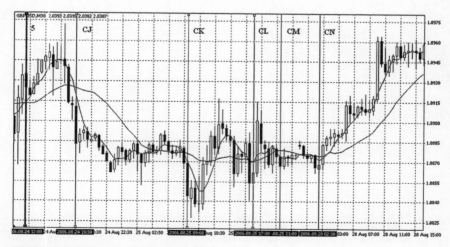

FIGURE 8.32 Crossovers August 24-28
Source: Copyright 2001–2007, MetaQuotes Software Corp.

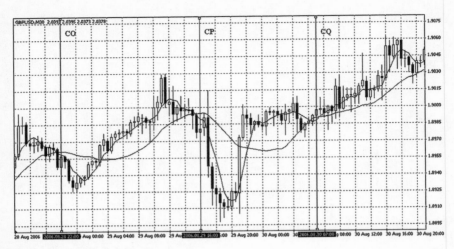

FIGURE 8.33 Crossovers August 28–30
Source: Copyright 2001–2007, MetaQuotes Software Corp.

Both of the crossover trade entries up in Figure 8.35 did not perform well. The CW entry would have been more severe because it would have been made with additional lots for cost averaging. Please keep in mind that this period of time was carefully selected to demonstrate the most difficult market conditions as the market swung wildly on the day chart. You can

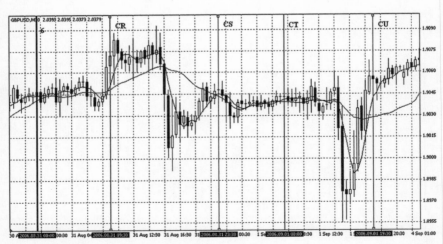

FIGURE 8.34 Crossovers August 30–September 1
Source: Copyright 2001–2007, MetaQuotes Software Corp.

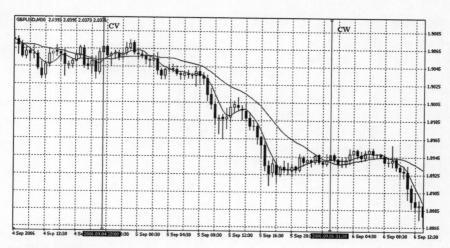

FIGURE 8.35 Crossovers September 4–5
Source: Copyright 2001–2007, MetaQuotes Software Corp.

examine the day chart and notice how it moves with the trend most of the time. These transitional times are the most treacherous, as you have seen.

So, if you can master trading under these conditions, then you will do very well under normal conditions.

Figure 8.36 shows opportunities for recovery with lines CX and CZ. The entry up to the right of line CY would be exited when the market reversed

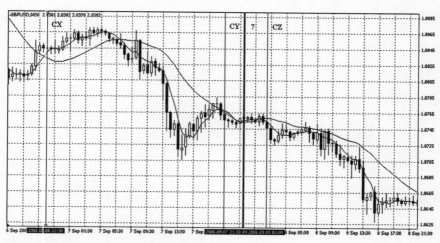

FIGURE 8.36 Crossovers September 6–8
Source: Copyright 2001–2007, MetaQuotes Software Corp.

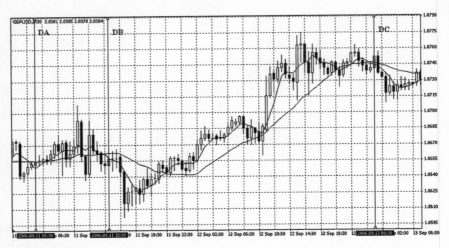

FIGURE 8.37 Crossovers September 11–12
Source: Copyright 2001–2007, MetaQuotes Software Corp.

upon entry. The bold line 7 represents the day chart cross in the downward direction.

Figure 8.37 shows three potential crossover trade entries down, the first of which retraced before paying profits. In fact, the DA entry represents one of the times where I will exit immediately. The DB entry paid over 40 pips before retracing upward. The DC entry shows a 30 pips move

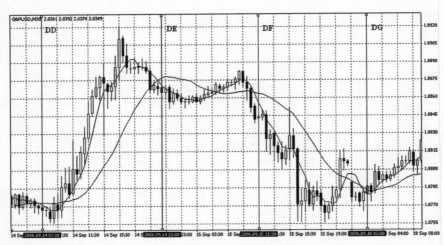

FIGURE 8.38 Crossovers September 14–15
Source: Copyright 2001–2007, MetaQuotes Software Corp.

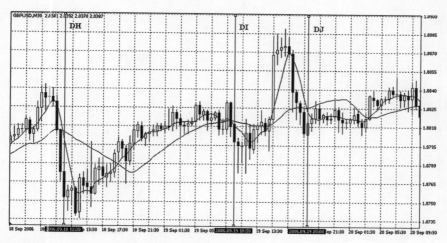

FIGURE 8.39 Crossovers September 18–19
Source: Copyright 2001–2007, MetaQuotes Software Corp.

right after the entry. This entry demonstrates how a better entry can result in waiting for the space to form to the left of the vertical line before entering the trade.

Figure 8.38 shows several crossover trade entries down beginning with DD, which did not work, but the stop-loss value was small. The next two

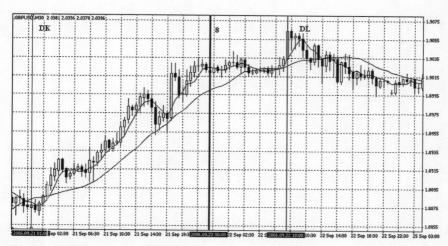

FIGURE 8.40 Crossovers September 21–22
Source. Copyright 2001–2007, MetaQuotes Software Corp.

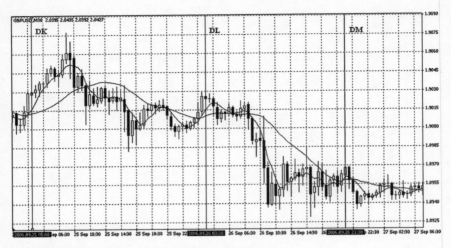

FIGURE 8.41 Crossovers September 25–26
Source: Copyright 2001–2007, MetaQuotes Software Corp.

trades did much better with additional lots. The trade to the right of line DG would be exited right away when the market moves upward.

Figure 8.39 also contains challenging trading conditions because the stop-loss values for entries DH and DJ are so large. You have learned by now that we can wait for better opportunities as they are presented. Once

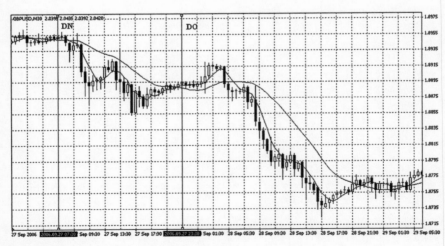

FIGURE 8.42 Crossovers September 27–28
Source: Copyright 2001–2007, MetaQuotes Software Corp.

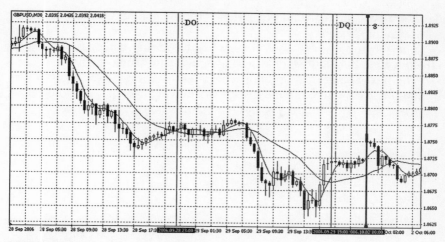

FIGURE 8.43 Crossovers September 28–29
Source: Copyright 2001–2007, MetaQuotes Software Corp.

again, let me remind you of this purposeful selection of tough trading conditions for you to study.

The crossover trade entries shown in Figure 8.40 at lines DK and DL reversed immediately resulting in a loss position. Once again, we see turbulence surrounding the change in the day direction.

The crossover entry up to the right of line DK in Figure 8.41 paid well, but the next one suffered a loss. The entry for line DM would be exited immediately when the reversal started. As you can see, the market is reversing rather dramatically following the cross up on the day chart. This is an extreme example.

Figure 8.42 begins with a flat market at line DN that does not merit an entry. The line DO does offer over 20 pips profit upward, however.

The first crossover entry up shown in Figure 8.43 at line DO gave about 15 pips profit, while the second gave over 40. Line 8 represents the next shift of the day chart as it crossed back down.

SUMMARY

This study included the various conditions that are presented to the trader by the Forex market. These conditions sometimes result in rather severe trading positions, as revealed in this study. The examples in this chapter demonstrate the difficulties the trader faces when attempting to use the cost average technique. This step-by-step process will assist you in developing the patience and confidence to understand how to persevere with a trading system.

The moving average tool is very helpful and is demonstrably more effective than the Slow Stochastic shown in the previous chapter.

The next chapter using Fibonacci ranges will show how to both use that tool and how to combine it with the moving average tool for what I think is a very powerful way to trade the Forex market.

CHAPTER 9

Loss Recovery with Fibonacci Ranges

The figures in this chapter will be similar to those of the last two using the GBP/USD currency combination. However, we will be examining the 30-minute time compression for moves in the direction of the trend as established from the day chart, following minor retracements on the 30-minute chart. These are very important moves in the market, and this chapter will be most helpful for you to understand the market anatomy and its dynamics. Figure 9.1 shows bold vertical lines where the market changed direction on the day chart during the summer of 2006. This figure is almost identical to the one in Chapter 8 that shows vertical lines where the two lines cross. The difference is that the vertical lines are drawn on this day chart when the five-candle moving average changes direction, and not when the two lines cross. This allows us to respond more quickly to the changes in the market direction. The two lines are the 5- and 20-candle simple moving average based upon the closing value of each candle.

We will examine the same period of June through September 2006 because of the difficulties encountered during those four months. Remember that this study is primarily intended for you to identify secondary market trades following your primary entries that are not working. You may ask, "Why not use these as primary entry points?" My answer is that it is good to trade anything that moves, as long as it works! So, you certainly have my permission.

Figure 9.1 looks very busy as the vertical lines show the changes in direction. Notice that some of these directional moves are very short-lived, while others take several days to complete. This example shows two moving average lines that will also be used on the 30-minute chart. They

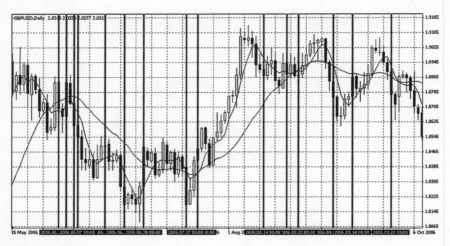

FIGURE 9.1 Day Chart Crossovers
Source: Copyright 2001–2007, MetaQuotes Software Corp.

are 5- and 20-candle simple averages based upon the closing values of the candles.

Figure 9.2 demonstrates the condition that I am looking for. Unfortunately the first setup to the right of the bold vertical line is not a good example, so I am showing you the final trade to the left before our study

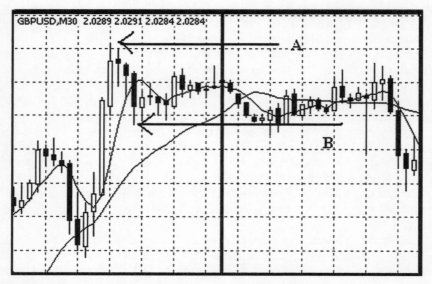

FIGURE 9.2 Range High and Low
Source: Copyright 2001–2007, MetaQuotes Software Corp.

begins. In this case we are looking for trades going down, and I have drawn two horizontal lines onto the chart showing a high point that was reached (A) and the low point to its right (B). The criterion for these points is the standard method for identifying resistance and support points. These points are determined by making sure that the wicks exceed those of its neighbors, two to the left and two to the right. It is a simple method that allows us to follow the market. So, you can see where the market moved up to line A, which is really a retracement because we are still looking for trades going down left of the vertical line. The market then returned downward and reached line B. We are interested in what happens next because the market often will make one more attempt at the retracement direction before returning to its previous trend.

In this example, the market did move back upward to the right of the line B arrow. The move upward was about half the distance between the two arrows. This is what I will be looking for during this entire study. This is called a 50 percent retracement. When this point is reached, it is significant but not totally trustworthy. When this point is reached, I wait for another resistance point to form with a wick that exceeds both its neighbors. So, on the third candle I plan to enter the market trading with the trend. You might be confused now, but after reviewing several of these you will understand it fully.

Figure 9.3 shows how I use the Fibonacci tool. I placed the cursor over the upper point and dragged the tool from that point to the low wick to the

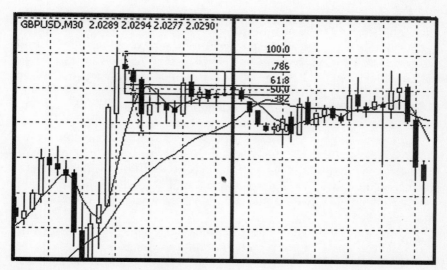

FIGURE 9.3 Range Fibonacci Values
Source: Copyright 2001–2007, MetaQuotes Software Corp.

right leaving a small dashed line connecting the two. The tool left in place six horizontal lines between the two points. I have set the tool to show just the major lines that I will use in this study. If you are already an expert in using this tool, please do not make fun of my settings, as I have left some out, and so on. I am concerned that if I show all of the Fibonacci points the examples will be so full of lines that it will be difficult to follow the main points I am trying to make. If you think that my lines are upside down, that is alright because it is a subjective decision.

This currency pair does not move as much as some others. Each currency pair has its own characteristics. The settings can be adjusted to each currency being studied, but it is important to use the Fibonacci ratio values. In this example I am waiting for the resistance point to be formed after the market reaches the 50 percent line. The entry down would be made on the third candle to the right of the first qualified resistance wick (higher than its neighbors, two to the left and two to the right) that reaches the 50 percent line. The trade stop value is just above the high wick, and the limit value is the low-wick value at line zero.

This is a very simple method. I always evaluate the position of the slow moving average line. If it is moving strongly against my direction, as in this example, I will not enter against it. You will find that during the large market moves, the market will offer false formations that can and should be avoided.

The first formation in Figure 9.4 for us to examine did not develop into an entry. After the 50 percent line was reached and the support point was established, the value of the support point was below the beginning support point. This is not good when trading up, and tells us that the market might not be ready to move upward.

When this happens, we need to wait for the next opportunity to trade where the slow moving average line is not moving severely against the potential trade direction. Because of the position of the slow moving average line, there are no other trade entry points on this figure.

With this first example you probably do not yet have a clue as to what we are doing. Well, just wait and go to the next one.

Figure 9.5 shows the only entry point for this short trend going down. Point A indicates the resistance (remember, two to the left and two to the right?), while Point B shows the support, and Point C shows the resistance point above the 50 percent line. Point D is where the profit point was reached going down. In this example the entry was at 1.8654 and the limit was 1.8630.

To the right of line 2, we begin looking for trades up. The formations to the right of the large move up do not offer any entries that we can use. If the third candle opens too far above the 50 percent line, then there is no room for profit, and we will wait for the next opportunity.

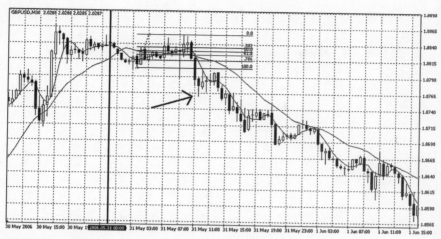

FIGURE 9.4 Crossover Entries and Targets May 30–31
Source: Copyright 2001–2007, MetaQuotes Software Corp.

The vertical line in Figure 9.6 shows the market changing direction yet again following the move up. We are now looking for reasons to enter down. Yes, this is the crazy Forex market that challenges every trading system. The entry down developed, and the entry point is shown by line A. The resulting 50 pips profit downward demonstrates the value of this

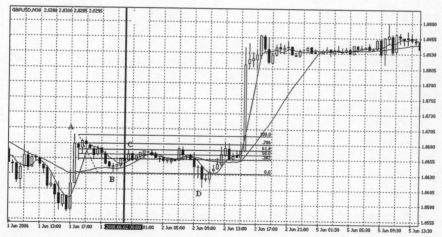

FIGURE 9.5 Crossover Entries and Targets June 1–5
Source: Copyright 2001–2007, MetaQuotes Software Corp.

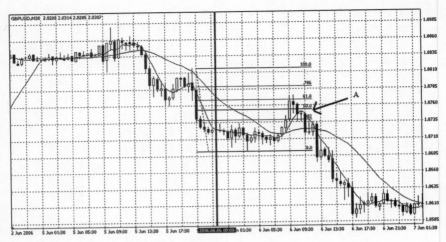

FIGURE 9.6 Crossover Entries and Targets June 5-6
Source: Copyright 2001-2007, MetaQuotes Software Corp.

method. So, do you get it? The trend is down. There is a small move up, so we enter the market going down, and we get our profit.

Notice that during the trade the moving average lines crossed. Chapter 8 illustrated the value of these crossings and showed how profitable they typically are. Using this method of cost averaging, we are already in the trade, and now have the opportunity of adding to our position at this time. This is a good example of how valuable this method really is.

Figure 9.7 shows a small trade just left of the vertical line. I would not recommend this trade because of the strong angle of the slow moving average line going against us.

The vertical line represents the next change in direction from the day chart, and the first qualifying entry is shown below to its right. This is another very good trade down as the profit was about 50 pips. I like this method because of its precision.

You can observe that another trade entry formed while the first one was still open. Under these conditions, I quite often will trade both and use the target from the latter for both trades. If the market conditions are changing, I want to be sure and accommodate it.

The next trade, as shown in Figure 9.8, is a beautiful one that rendered another 50 pips down. As soon as a support formation is completed (two to the left and two to the right) I draw the Fibonacci lines and wait to see if the market comes back to the 50 percent line. If it does NOT come back that far, then no trade can be entered down at that time. If it does come back, then I will enter down as soon as it hits that 50 percent value.

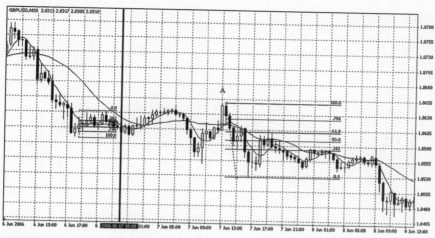

FIGURE 9.7 Crossover Entries and Targets June 6–7
Source: Copyright 2001–2007, MetaQuotes Software Corp.

Notice that the retracement exceeded the 50 percent line and reached the 61.8 line. When this happens, I am already in the trade, so I adjust the limit or profit target accordingly and settle for less profit. If the market is telling us that it is interested in going up, then I will not expect it to reach my target with the same momentum. I would rather take less profit than suffer a loss.

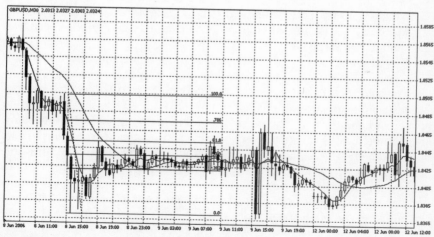

FIGURE 9.8 Crossover Entries and Targets June 8–9
Source: Copyright 2001–2007, MetaQuotes Software Corp.

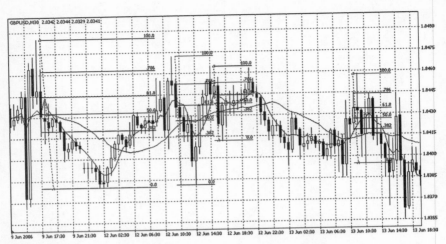

FIGURE 9.9 Crossover Entries and Targets June 9–13
Source: Copyright 2001–2007, MetaQuotes Software Corp.

The three trades shown in Figure 9.9 are all worth trading, but there are some rules that I follow. The first trade reaches the .786 line, so I would reduce my profit expectations and not expect the market to reach the 0.0 line. The second trade forms and also has a .786 retracement, so once again I adjust my limit. The third trade forms as the second one is closing, and it is smaller than the earlier two.

The fourth trade shows additional profits, making it a very good trading day. This is a pretty picture that shows how this method works for you.

The entry on the left side of Figure 9.10 shows a good trade down that gave about 30 pips profit.

Notice the retracement in the center of the chart that I have not used because of the moving average slow line angle going up so sharply.

The trade down on the right is not a good one, and resulted in a loss. An experienced trader would change the profit point on the first trade when the second one formed. The second trade had not yet paid when the third one formed. I would close the second trade at the target for the third trade. Because the market spiked above the initial resistance point, the third formation is not fully qualified, and a trade entry is not indicated. But, I would still use its target for the previous trade.

The entries to the right of the vertical line as shown in Figure 9.11 occur one after the other in quick succession. Unfortunately the first two are not profitable, while the third gives only about 10 pips. In examining these trades, the second and third should not be entered because the moving average slow line had a severe angle. The unmarked formation on the right

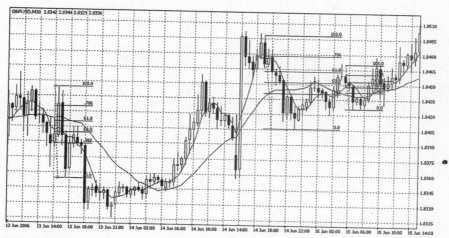

FIGURE 9.10 Crossover Entries and Targets June 13–14
Source: Copyright 2001–2007, MetaQuotes Software Corp.

is not drawn because the entry point candle reached below the starting candle. In this case you should exit quickly. Notice also how fast the slow moving average line formed a sharp angle against the last unmarked trade.

The leftmost two-line sets on Figure 9.12 are interesting because the first support point to the right of the candle that struck the 50 percent line is well below our starting point, thus letting us know not to enter here.

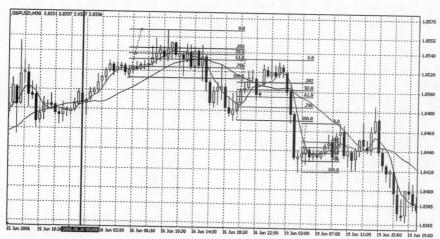

FIGURE 9.11 Crossover Entries and Targets June 15–19
Source: Copyright 2001–2007, MetaQuotes Software Corp.

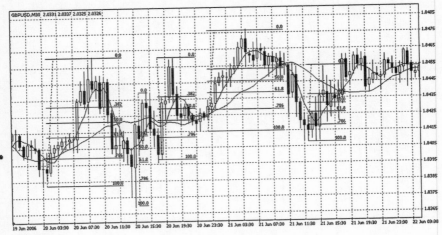

FIGURE 9.12 Crossover Entries and Targets June 20–21
Source: Copyright 2001–2007, MetaQuotes Software Corp.

The second formation entry point is too close to the target. I would, therefore, not enter either of these first two formations.

The third formation traded beautifully.

The fourth formation goes below the starting support point demonstrating why I set my stop value at least 10 pips below the entry. The market will at times return to the starting point where the bankers and brokers grab our stops. So, I leave a little room for the market to breathe. The rightmost formation does not form correctly after the 50 percent line is reached, which would prevent us from entering at that time so close to the target.

Figure 9.13 shows the vertical line indicating that the day chart has crossed down again.

The first trade entry down does not reach the 50 percent line until the second entry has closed. This is the condition where I would close both positions when the target for the second one is reached.

The rightmost formation also met its target going down.

The first two formations in Figure 9.14 did not develop for trade entries because of the spikes above the initial resistance point, but the other two did very well moving downward.

The two trade entries down on Figure 9.15 were both successful. The major announcement resulting in the large candle would result in a loss if it was traded when it hit the 50 percent line that is not drawn. I would not attempt to enter a trade under these conditions, and would wait for a better choice with a higher probability of success.

The vertical line indicates a change in trading direction from the day chart. We will now look for trades going up.

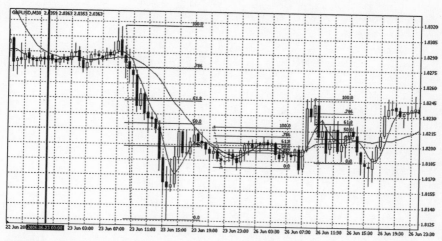

FIGURE 9.13 Crossover Entries and Targets June 23–26
Source: Copyright 2001–2007, MetaQuotes Software Corp.

The first formation in Figure 9.16 broke below the starting point while forming the resistance point, so there was no upward trade indicated. The second formation did not reach the 50 percent line, so no entry was possible there also. The next three formations were better and performed well going up. The last up entry on the right did not reach the target, but because the resistance point formation reached below .786, the target should be

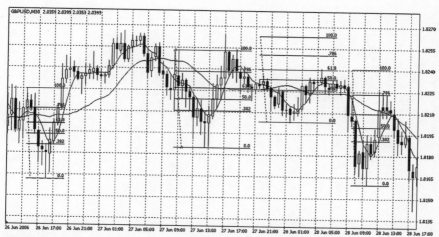

FIGURE 9.14 Crossover Entries and Targets June 28–26
Source: Copyright 2001–2007, MetaQuotes Software Corp.

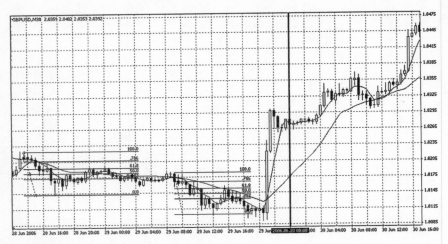

FIGURE 9.15 Crossover Entries and Targets June 28–29
Source: Copyright 2001–2007, MetaQuotes Software Corp.

adjusted downward anyway, which would allow for successful closure of the trade prior to the large retracement downward.

Figure 9.17 contains one very good entry up before the larger move up, followed by three formations that were either not tradeable or did not work. The first to the right of the move up did not make profit and suffered

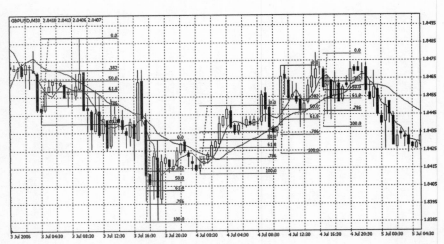

FIGURE 9.16 Crossover Entries and Targets July 3–4
Source: Copyright 2001–2007, MetaQuotes Software Corp.

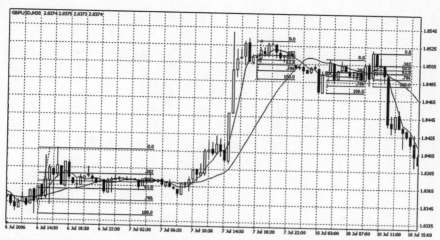

FIGURE 9.17 Crossover Entries and Targets July 6–7
Source: Copyright 2001–2007, MetaQuotes Software Corp.

a minor loss. The next was too close to the target when the third candle opened right of the support point (remember, two to the left and two to the right must be higher). The rightmost formation fell below the starting point before the support point was formed, rendering the formation untradeable.

In Figure 9.18, the first three formations up paid nicely. The fourth did not clear before the fifth closed, and the fifth retraced down nearly to the

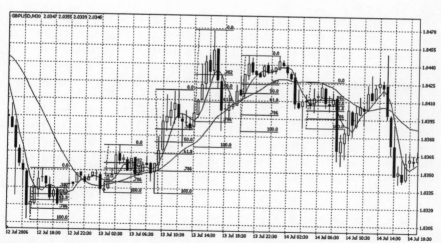

FIGURE 9.18 Crossover Entries and Targets July 12–14
Source: Copyright 2001–2007, MetaQuotes Software Corp.

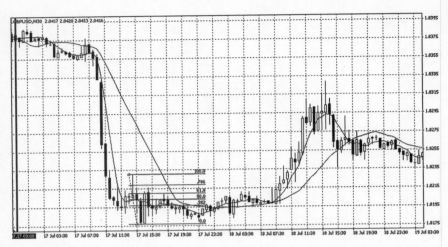

FIGURE 9.19 Crossover Entries and Targets July 17–18
Source: Copyright 2001–2007, MetaQuotes Software Corp.

starting point, which lowers my expectations. I would close the fifth trade with minimal profits and close the fourth trade at the same time.

The sixth formation up resulted in no entry as the market went below the starting point while forming the required support bird.

The seventh opportunity up did the same thing as the market dropped before the support bird was formed. I did not draw a Fibonacci range for that formation.

The bold vertical line on the left of Figure 9.19 is telling us that the day chart moving average crossed down. So we begin to trade in that direction.

The large move down did not form a retracement pattern allowing us to get in on the move. The movement at the bottom retraced for one entry down that did not fully develop, and a loss might have ensued depending upon the target and the skill of the trader.

The day chart cross down did not have much commitment and reversed itself almost immediately. This condition is the one that I have purposely chosen for you to study with me because of its difficulties. There was a loss in the previous figure, and here, in Figure 9.20, there are two small gains. These are very dangerous waters, but this method is still serving well.

The entry on the right cleared as the target was met before the large move up.

To the right of the vertical line in Figure 9.21 we begin looking for trades up, and we find three. The market made an attempt to change the trend in the previous three days, but changed direction and continued

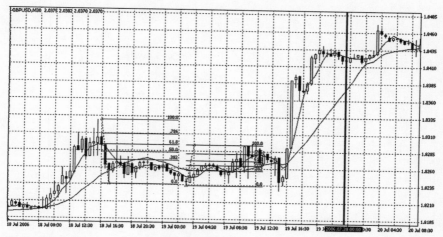

FIGURE 9.20 Crossover Entries and Targets July 18–19
Source: Copyright 2001–2007, MetaQuotes Software Corp.

upward. We can see the nice move upward and how this method was able to take advantage of the situation.

The patterns in Figure 9.22 are the most interesting in this entire chapter. Here we have a market moving down while we are trying to trade up. To the left you can see the large move up and its corresponding retracement

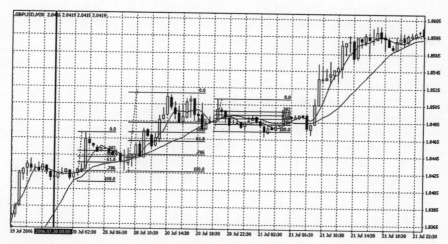

FIGURE 9.21 Crossover Entries and Targets July 20–21
Source: Copyright 2001–2007, MetaQuotes Software Corp.

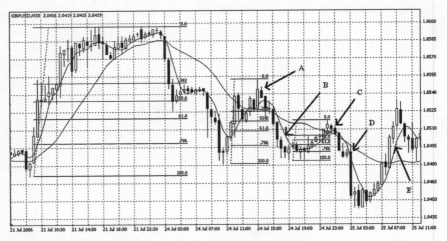

FIGURE 9.22 Crossover Entries and Targets July 21–25
Source: Copyright 2001–2007, MetaQuotes Software Corp.

to the 50 percent mark. Because the moving average lines have so much angle and separation, I would not enter the market until I see them cross upward (see line A). The market then immediately reversed against the trade, and I would exit the trade with a loss at line B when the moving average lines re-crossed. This would allow for a savings of a few pips short of the entry point.

The second formation is almost identical to the first. The entry at line C was delayed due to the moving average angle and separation against the trade. Line C is where the moving average lines finally crossed up indicating some market commitment in that direction. Unfortunately, the market fell as soon as the trade was entered, but the re-crossing of the lines is the signal to bail out of the trade and wait for the next cycle to reenter. Whew, now that is tough! This is about as bad as it gets. These were three difficult trades in a row, but now that you should understand the game plan, it is not discouraging or disabling. We understand the rules, and patiently wait for the market to come back to us with its dance.

Yes, I am increasing the lots as I go on with these trades, because I know that the market will either return to normalcy or the day chart direction will change again allowing me to also change direction.

The leftmost entry in Figure 9.23 in our short series of losses is the worst because the stop-loss value is reached before the moving average lines cross against the trade. We now have four consecutive losses, and the worst that you will see in this period of three months. The challenge when trading the Forex is to minimize the losses in order to emerge with

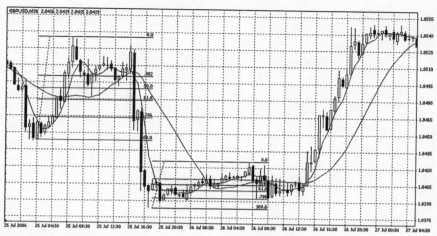

FIGURE 9.23 Crossover Entries and Targets July 25–26
Source: Copyright 2001–2007, MetaQuotes Software Corp.

an overall gain. Our attempt to exit quickly gives us an advantage in these situations. Yes, my fourth entry would have been with additional lots to start the recovery process and not miss the market reversal. What makes me upset is when the reversal occurs without my participation!

The smaller trade upward to the right was successful and limited in its scope. But at least we see the market returning to the correct direction. Whew!

Figure 9.24 shows the recovery process at work with two successful trading opportunities up. The first formation contains a smaller one within it, but the entry candle two to the right of the one that struck the 50 percent line was already at the target, so a trade would not be made.

The four trades up shown in Figure 9.25 performed very well. This should be routine for you at this point.

Figure 9.26 shows the market entering a lamb condition where it moved slightly during a two-day period. There are two formations in the middle of the chart, the first of which did not pay, but the second of which did pay. As you know, I prefer to close both entries when the second one clears. This is a precaution that pays dividends in the long run, and this is an example where the market was giving us a sign that it is not certain of the direction. The stop-loss value would have been reached on the first trade.

You can plainly see the Fibonacci retracement for the large move up in the middle of the chart compared to the beginning low point to the left and the retracement to the right. I do not attempt to trade such large moves

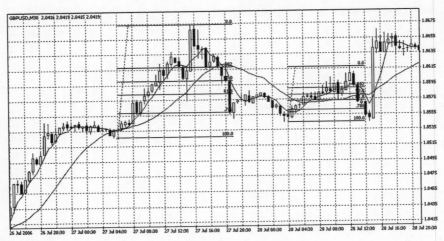

FIGURE 9.24 Crossover Entries and Targets July 26–28
Source: Copyright 2001–2007, MetaQuotes Software Corp.

on this time compression. If I am interested in these moves, I will trade from the 60-minute chart where the horizontal distance will be smaller and where I can view a more accurate assessment of the market stops and limits.

The two formations in Figure 9.27 are sandwiched between the large entries up and, unfortunately, do not allow us to get most of the moves.

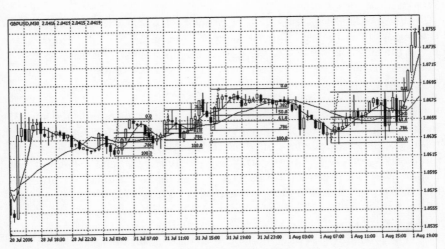

FIGURE 9.25 Crossover Entries and Targets July 28–31
Source: Copyright 2001–2007, MetaQuotes Software Corp.

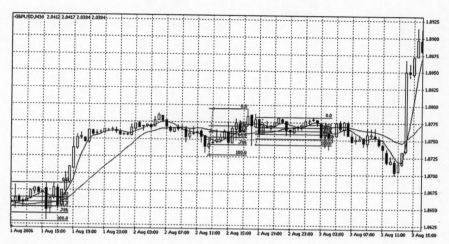

FIGURE 9.26 Crossover Entries and Targets August 1-2
Source: Copyright 2001-2007, MetaQuotes Software Corp.

But, that is alright because the large moves that result from economic announcements are so very dangerous and unpredictable.

Both of these formations met the target, although I would not enter the second one, but would have adjusted the target for the first one downward for safety.

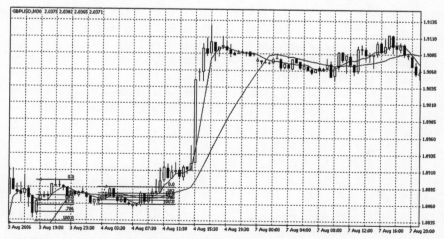

FIGURE 9.27 Crossover Entries and Targets August 3-7
Source: Copyright 2001-2007, MetaQuotes Software Corp.

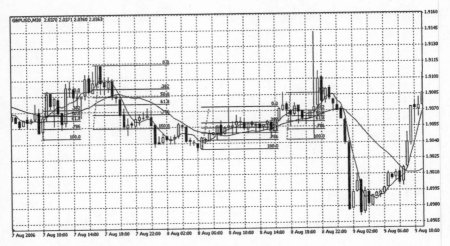

FIGURE 9.28 Crossover Entries and Targets August 7–8
Source: Copyright 2001–2007, MetaQuotes Software Corp.

Figure 9.28 shows four entry opportunities up. The leftmost was too close to the target when the support point was formed, so no trade could be made.

The second one formed its support point below the beginning support point, so no trade was merited there either.

The third formation was a good one for a small profit.

The fourth is using the support point from the third as its entry and the high to its left as the target, which was reached before the market went down.

The first trade entry on Figure 9.29 was too close to the target upon completion of the support point, so no trade would be entered. The second formation support point was below the initial support point, so no trade would be entered there also.

The formations to the right of the lines I have drawn do not allow for entries because the support points develop below the starting support point.

The first trade entry drawn on Figure 9.30 was too close to the target by the time the support point was fully formed.

The second would not be traded due to the low support point.

The third formation also required an adjustment of its target due to the deep retracement.

These deep retracements are telling us that the market is looking for a reason to reverse itself.

The bold vertical line, as shown in Figure 9.31, represents the cross on the day chart to let us know that we should be looking for trades going down.

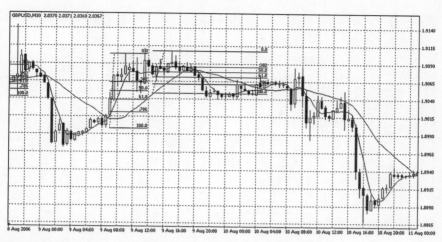

FIGURE 9.29 Crossover Entries and Targets August 9–10
Source: Copyright 2001–2007, MetaQuotes Software Corp.

The first entry down to the right of the vertical line had a large retracement, so the target should be adjusted accordingly, but still might not have cleared before the second trade did. In any event, one or both trades in Figure 9.31 were successful.

Figure 9.32 shows the small trade down following the large move upward. The trade to its right is much more dramatic and paid larger profits,

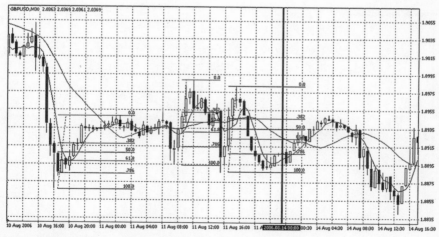

FIGURE 9.30 Crossover Entries and Targets August 10–11
Source: Copyright 2001–2007, MetaQuotes Software Corp.

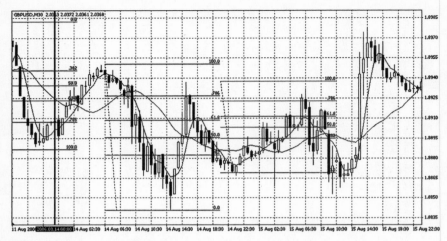

FIGURE 9.31   Crossover Entries and Targets August 14–15
Source: Copyright 2001–2007, MetaQuotes Software Corp.

although its target merited adjustment due to the retracement above the
.618 level.

Figure 9.33 shows three formations that look good until you measure
the data and discover that by the time the resistance points are completed
the market is too close to the target, or the resistance point itself is too
high. So, there are no good entries on this figure.

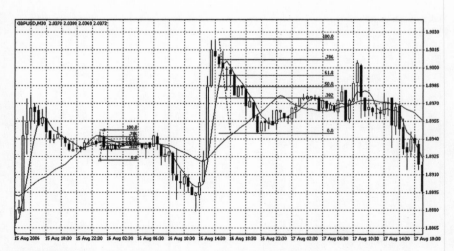

FIGURE 9.32   Crossover Entries and Targets August 15–16
Source: Copyright 2001–2007, MetaQuotes Software Corp.

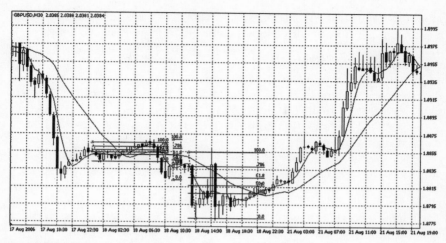

FIGURE 9.33 Crossover Entries and Targets August 17–18
Source: Copyright 2001–2007, MetaQuotes Software Corp.

One good thing to be said about trading with these tools is that very seldom will you get caught in one of these large moves going in the wrong direction. I have met many traders who say that they trade well until they are caught in a large move going the wrong way that takes back all of their earnings. So, if we can avoid that condition it gives us an advantage.

The bold vertical line near the left margin in Figure 9.34 indicates the change in trading direction as determined by the day chart when the

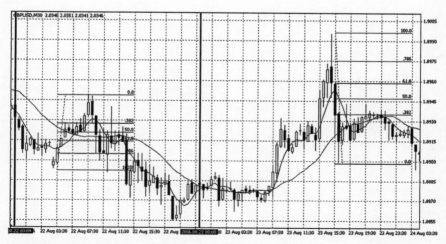

FIGURE 9.34 Crossover Entries and Targets August 22–23
Source: Copyright 2001–2007, MetaQuotes Software Corp.

moving average line changed direction. This figure shows the beginning of a turbulent period when the market changed directions several times.

The formation on the left did not develop because the support point was lower than its initial one.

The formation drawn on the right did not reach the 50 percent line, but the move was so large that the retracement only reached the .382 level, so the target could actually be adjusted to a larger number.

Figure 9.35 shows two formations going down, the first of which worked very well.

The second entry resistance point was too high, so no trade is indicated. But, I would definitely enter the trade when the moving average lines crossed downward. This is a condition that I always look for as a secondary entry. So, in this case I could be cost averaging my cost-average trade.

Figure 9.36 shows two trade entries down to the left of the vertical line, the first of which retraced above the entry line, so I would not enter a trade. I would enter when the moving average lines crossed down, however. The second also came close to the entry line, so I would reduce the target accordingly.

Target reductions are not exact pip for pip, so I generally am conservative and reduce my target a little more than necessary to make sure that I get something out of the trade and try to avoid a loss.

To the right of the vertical line there are two formations for trade entries up. You may have noticed that I will look left of a vertical line to obtain the starting point of a new formation for a trade entry in the new direction.

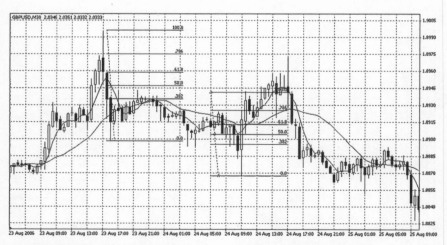

FIGURE 9.35 Crossover Entries and Targets August 23–24
Source: Copyright 2001–2007, MetaQuotes Software Corp.

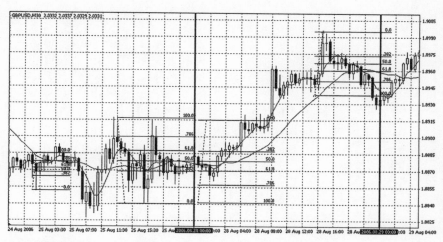

FIGURE 9.36 Crossover Entries and Targets August 25–28
Source: Copyright 2001–2007, MetaQuotes Software Corp.

In this case, we have an entry develop when the support point was formed. Keep in mind that the starting point is quite often the support point from the previous formation.

The fourth formation formed its second support point below the first, rendering it untradeable unless the moving average lines cross, which did occur here. While this formation was building, the day chart indicated yet another change in direction, but as you can see, the trade up still fulfilled its duties and met the target.

Figure 9.37 shows another short trend as the day chart reversed itself again. The leftmost formation is the last one reviewed in the previous figure.

The second formation is a nice entry down that paid very well. But, the next one did not provide a profit as it reversed to follow the new trend. By the time the resistance point was formed, however, the moving average lines had severe angle and separation going against the trade, so I would not enter until those lines crossed going down. Because they recrossed almost immediately, I would have closed the trade with a minimal loss.

The rightmost formation also paid nicely.

Figure 9.38 contains two formations that met their targets as expected. Between them is a malformed one that did not allow for an entry because the support point formed well below the start line.

The trade entry up shown in Figure 9.39 is the only one that formed before the large move downward.

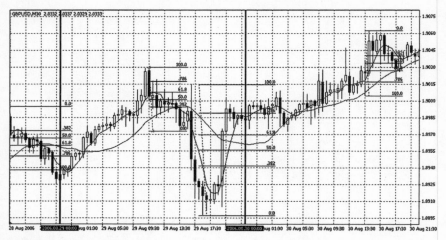

FIGURE 9.37 Crossover Entries and Targets August 28–29
Source: Copyright 2001–2007, MetaQuotes Software Corp.

The entry in Figure 9.40 shows an unusual well-formed market that nearly reached the 50 percent line before moving to the target. The trade to its right also went to the target with minimal resistance. Because the resistance point was formed below the .382 line, I would move the target down for added profits. Entering cost average trades under these conditions is quite exciting.

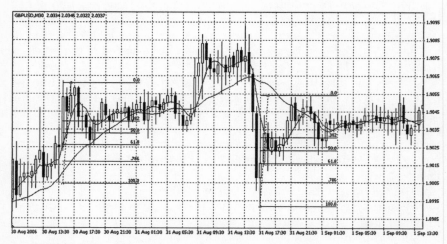

FIGURE 9.38 Crossover Entries and Targets August 30–31
Source: Copyright 2001–2007, MetaQuotes Software Corp.

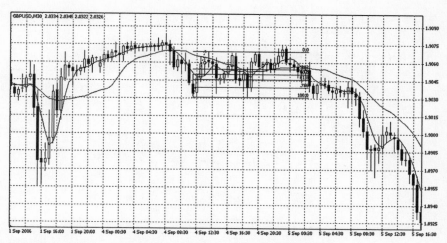

FIGURE 9.39 Crossover Entries and Targets September 1–5
Source: Copyright 2001–2007, MetaQuotes Software Corp.

Notice the vertical line on the left indicating another change in direction as the day chart lines crossed down.

Figure 9.41 begins with three formations down, all of which worked well. The second did not clear until the third did, and remember that I will clear the second at the target for the third.

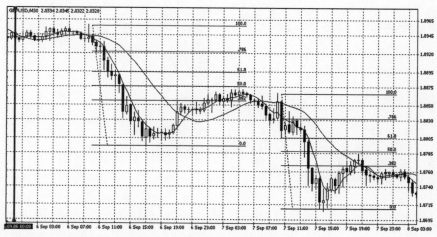

FIGURE 9.40 Crossover Entries and Targets September 6–7
Source: Copyright 2001–2007, MetaQuotes Software Corp.

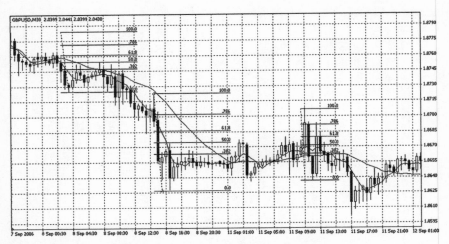

FIGURE 9.41 Crossover Entries and Targets September 8–11
Source: Copyright 2001–2007, MetaQuotes Software Corp.

The first down entry shown in Figure 9.42 is a good one, but the second does not achieve profit before the stop value is reached.

The vertical line indicates that the day chart has reversed direction upward.

Both of the up entries shown in Figure 9.43 are successful, but, the second one might have reached our stop-loss value, which I always place 20-plus pips below the entry.

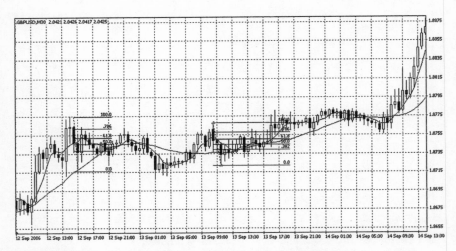

FIGURE 9.42 Crossover Entries and Targets September 12–13
Source: Copyright 2001–2007, MetaQuotes Software Corp.

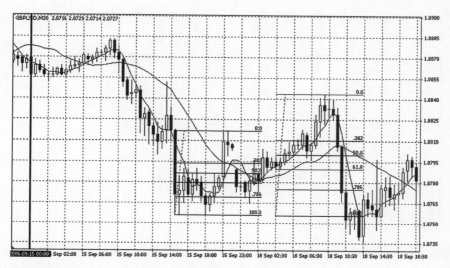

FIGURE 9.43 Crossover Entries and Targets September 15–18
Source: Copyright 2001–2007, MetaQuotes Software Corp.

Figure 9.44 shows one large formation that did very well.

The entry shown on Figure 9.45 shows another trade entry up that performed very well.

Figure 9.46 shows another sweet entry up after the retracement that paid nicely.

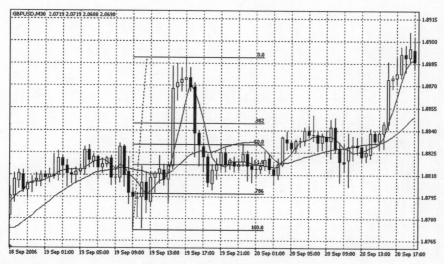

FIGURE 9.44 Crossover Entries and Targets September 18–19
Source: Copyright 2001–2007, MetaQuotes Software Corp.

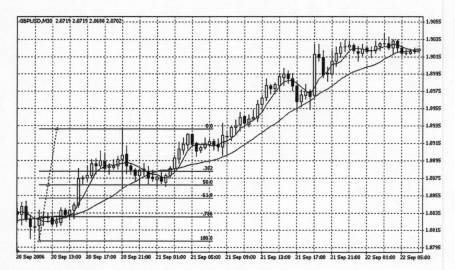

FIGURE 9.45 Crossover Entries and Targets September 20–22
Source: Copyright 2001–2007, MetaQuotes Software Corp.

Both of the entries up for Figure 9.47 were good after adjusting the target for the first one after the second one formed.

The single entry on September 27, as shown in Figure 9.48, was not successful as the retracement turned into a reversal against the trend instead of returning to the target as indicated by the chart formation.

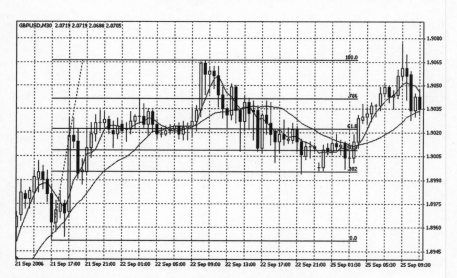

FIGURE 9.46 Crossover Entries and Targets September 25–26
Source: Copyright 2001–2007, MetaQuotes Software Corp.

FIGURE 9.47 Crossover Entries and Targets September 26–28
Source: Copyright 2001–2007, MetaQuotes Software Corp.

In the next chapter you will learn how I make profits when the market does this.

The two moves up with retracements in this last example in this study were also successful.

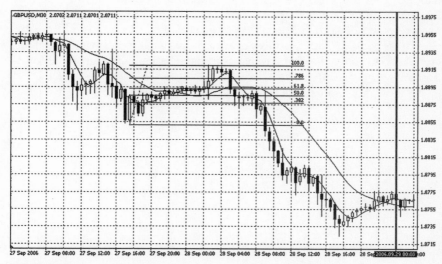

FIGURE 9.48 Crossover Entries and Targets September 27–28
Source: Copyright 2001–2007, MetaQuotes Software Corp.

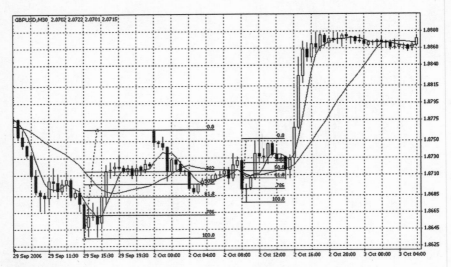

FIGURE 9.49 Crossover Entries and Targets September 29–October 2
Source: Copyright 2001–2007, MetaQuotes Software Corp.

SUMMARY

This study, as I have stated previously, covers the most difficult market transitions that I could find for the GBP/USD currency pair. But, as you can see from the various entries and exits, this methodology of using the Fibonacci and moving average indicators is about the most effective market analysis tool set that I have discussed so far.

These tools provide the most accurate assessment of the market at any given time to assist the trader to use the cost average technique to maintain positive trading results.

But, wait. Chapter 10 is even better! Let's go!

Loss Recovery
with Trend Lines

T he figures in this chapter will be similar to those of the last ones using the GBP/USD currency combination. However, we will be examining the 30-minute time compression for moves in the direction of the trend as established from the four-hour chart, following minor retracements on the 30-minute chart. These are also very important moves in the market, and this chapter will be most helpful for you to understand more about the market anatomy and its dynamics.

The process used in this chapter will be very similar to the past as we examine the four-hour chart and draw bold vertical lines to the right of each and every change in direction of the five-candle simple moving average (SMA) line. Figure 10.1 shows the beginning of our study during the summer of 2006.

I have stated previously that this period of June through September 2006 is best because of the difficulties encountered during those four months. Remember that this study is primarily intended for you to identify secondary market trades following your primary entries that are not working.

Figure 10.1 looks very busy because there are several tools being used at the same time. Let me describe them for you. The bold vertical line on the right is telling us that the four-hour chart changed to the down direction at that time, but to its left we will consider only trading up.

Using trend lines for trading with this methodology is quite simple as we look for support points to the left and support points to the right. The idea is to connect each major support point, and then to extend the line

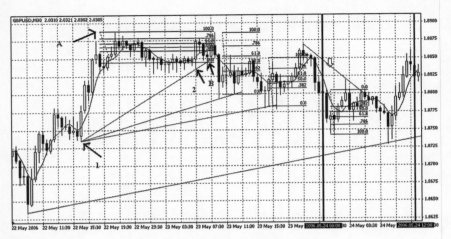

FIGURE 10.1 Crossover Entries and Targets May 22–23
Source: Copyright 2001–2007, MetaQuotes Software Corp.

to the right until a wick hits it. I am referring exclusively to support points because we are only interested in trading up at this time. When a wick strikes a trend line, a buy trade can be entered presuming that a bounce off the support point will develop. The stop-loss value is determined by the most appropriate support point to the left, and it is subjective for the trader to choose. If the closest one is a large number of pips away, then it might be best to not enter. As you read this chapter you will develop an understanding of the decision process and the risk-reward issues. Once the stop-loss value is selected, the target can also be evaluated. I use the Fibonacci tool for this task by drawing the range from the most appropriate "resistance point" to the left to the trade entry point. The target is typically the .618 area within the range. You might want to use the 100.0 line, but the market quite often will challenge but not reach the previous resistance level leaving you with an open trade and a great deal of stress and, not to mention, less profit!

Figure 10.1 shows point 1 as the origin for the trend line, point 2 as the fulcrum, and point B as the destination where the candle wick strikes it. Point A is the range top for the Fibonacci measurement, and point B is the bottom. In this example the entry is approximately 1.8844. The target is 1.8878. The stop value is 1.8827 (support to the left) or 1.8735, which is the origin of the trend line. I am generally not very nervous about large stop-loss values, because the market will usually give us a reason to exit the trade before such a large loss is made. Trades can be exited when another trade in the same direction has a smaller stop-loss value and target or when it is going in the other direction.

In the case of the first trade on Figure 10.1, you can see that the target was not reached before another trade was called for. The second trade entry is 1.8799 with a target of 1.8867 and a stop-loss value of 1.8735. Before the target is reached for the second trade, a third trade entry is presented with an entry value of 1.8782, a target of 1.8835, and a stop-loss value of 1.8735. The third trade reaches its target in short order, at which time I would exit all three trades. This would result in a loss of 9 pips for the first trade, a gain of 36 pips for the second, and a gain of 53 pips for the third, which would bring the total to 98 pips altogether. The decision to exit all three trades is letting the market advise me about its intentions, and helping me to scale back the targets that were previously selected.

In Chapter 9 we used the Fibonacci tool extensively, so you are familiar with it at this point. The settings can be varied for different currency combinations that might be more or less responsive. In this book I am using just a few to help to avoid cluttered formations.

To the right of the vertical line there is just one trade opportunity with an entry of 1.8804 and a target of 1.8756 that was reached within a few hours.

There, that was easy, right? These are easy tools and formations to look for. Drawing these lines is not difficult, and it is easy to practice this method using historical data.

Figure 10.2 contains five sections for each time the four-hour chart direction changed. The first section contains three small trades down that were successful: the first for 17 pips profit with a 17-pip stop value, the

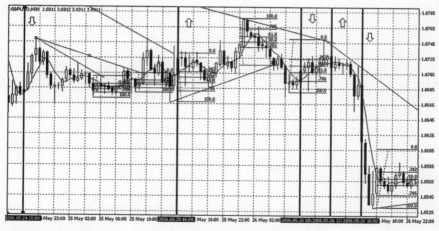

FIGURE 10.2 Crossover Entries and Targets May 25–26
Source: Copyright 2001–2007, MetaQuotes Software Corp.

second for about 10 pips profit with a 20-pip stop value, and the last for about 41 pips profit with a 20-pip stop value.

The second section contains just one trade with a 48-pip target and a 60-pip stop-loss value. But, before the trade reaches either position the next signal develops in the opposite direction. When this occurs, I close the older trade and go with the new one. In this case it is a trade down for about 50 pips profit using a 30-pip stop value. The earlier trade would close with about 30 pips profit also.

The trade in the rightmost section will be discussed in Figure 10.3.

Remember that these lines have three contact points consisting of the origin, the fulcrum or pivot, and the destination. When the market reaches the destination a bounce should occur in the direction of the trend.

Figure 10.3 shows a large move down followed by a slight retracement. This condition occurs frequently, and the market generally continues moving in the direction of the large move decisively or reverses direction slowly. The target for this trade is about 50 pips, while the stop-loss value is well over 100 pips. Under these conditions, I would not enter in either direction.

Figure 8.2 in Chapter 8 shows the same trade down in the middle of the chart underscoring the importance of using all of the tools at your disposal. If you were looking to cost average going up, you would need to wait for the market turn at 16:00 on May 29. But, if you were looking for a reason to enter down, then the techniques discussed in Chapter 8 would be best suited.

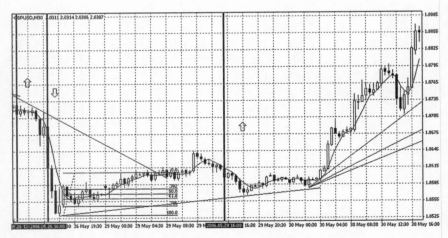

FIGURE 10.3 Crossover Entries and Targets May 26–30
Source: Copyright 2001–2007, MetaQuotes Software Corp.

It is important to use all of these tools in order to use every opportunity to your advantage. This book is organized for this purpose.

The first formation in Figure 10.4 is quite a bit left of the trend line strike, but it is a good trade entry of about 1.8813 with a 40-pip target and a 25-pip stop value.

The second trade up enters at 1.8811, and before it reaches the target, another trade entry is reached at 1.8763 with a new target of 1.8837. Unfortunately, the market goes against both trades, and I would exit both at the first stop-loss value of 1.8759 minus 20 pips.

The third trade is in the new direction and enters at 1.8750 with about a 10-pip target that is easily reached.

Figure 10.5 shows the market moving down and providing us with five little retracements along the way where we can make money. It is amazing how fast these small transactions add up to large amounts of earnings.

You might look at this chart and think that it would be better to stay in the trade and get all the money, but only experienced and advanced traders can predict the future behavior of the Forex.

I am very happy to make 10–20 pips at a time during these larger moves. Using the Fibonacci ratios, I will occasionally stay in a larger trade, but it is easier to sleep at night when no trades are open.

The vertical line in Figure 10.6 shows where the recovery began on the four-hour chart. The large move up developed in the middle of our trade. This is another example of the technical formations giving us a clear indication of where the smart money is. Prior to this large move up, the insiders

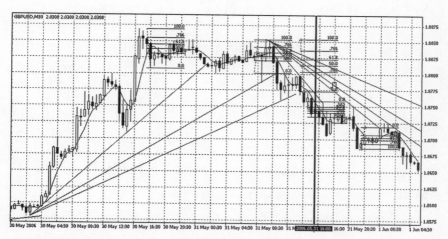

FIGURE 10.4 Crossover Entries and Targets May 30–31
Source: Copyright 2001–2007, MetaQuotes Software Corp.

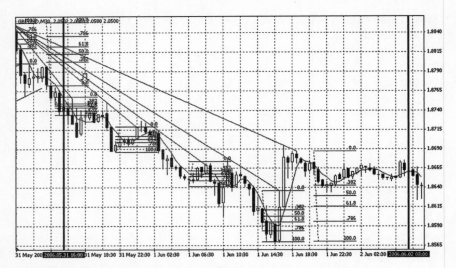

FIGURE 10.5   Crossover Entries and Targets May 31–June 1
Source: Copyright 2001–2007, MetaQuotes Software Corp.

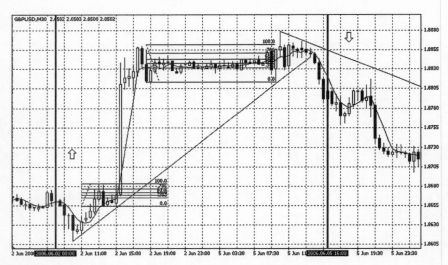

FIGURE 10.6   Crossover Entries and Targets June 2–5
Source: Copyright 2001–2007, MetaQuotes Software Corp.

FIGURE 10.7 Crossover Entries and Targets June 5-7
Source: Copyright 2001-2007, MetaQuotes Software Corp.

and bankers with advanced knowledge began to move their money quietly, and the market responded. After the fact we can easily see the move, but before the fact it is not enough for me to trade. I always rely on the technical interpretation of candlestick formations for my trading decisions.

Figure 10.7 shows only one trade for June 6 where the market retraced over 75 pips to let us into the market going back down. This is a wonderful picture.

The next three trades as shown in Figure 10.8 are a continuation of the move down. There is one important thing to see on this chart as the breakouts give a clue to more profit potential.

I look for the formations where the market reaches a low point, retraces for three to fifteen candles, and then challenges the previous low again. If the previous high is not too far away, I will use it for the stop-loss value and then trade the break below the previous low for 10–20 pips. Notice how effective it would work on this chart.

Not only do I trade to the Fibonacci target, but I will also stay in the trade for more profits when these formations develop.

In these examples below, the retracement was severe and went above the basis line, and many times when this happens I will then decline to trade the formation. But, in these cases the breakouts are compelling. I might not even enter until the breakout below the previous low occurs.

The first trade shown in Figure 10.9 is already at the target when the resistance is formed, but the market breaks out below the newly formed

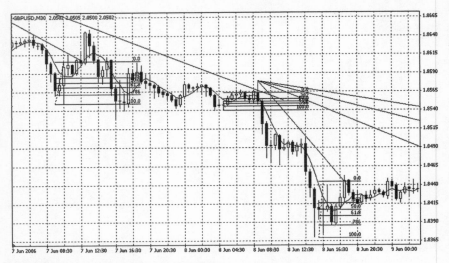

FIGURE 10.8 Crossover Entries and Targets June 7–8
Source: Copyright 2001–2007, MetaQuotes Software Corp.

FIGURE 10.9 Crossover Entries and Targets June 9–12
Source: Copyright 2001–2007, MetaQuotes Software Corp.

low, which allows us to enter at that time. Under these conditions, I will often place a pending order for the broker to enter at the specific market value so I do not have to always be watching the dealing station when the market moves.

The second trade formation is a better one as there is room for profits when the market strikes the trend line. Because the four-hour fast moving average line was about to turn upward, I probably would decline to enter this trade. This is a condition that I check before each trade is entered.

The third trade is now in the upward direction and is a wonderful profit-making venture.

The entry on the left side of Figure 10.10 shows an easy entry with good profits plus a breakout for a bonus.

The second entry is not a good one, and the retracement would be close to the stop-loss value, which would cause me to adjust the target to be less aggressive. Again, because the four-hour fast moving average line is changing direction, I would maybe not enter at that point.

The third entry is a very good one, as it is a large move and it also includes a good breakout opportunity.

The first three entries shown on Figure 10.11 move to the target before the support formation is fully formed, but in each case the breakout above the previous high renders profits.

The fourth trade is an excellent one, and the breakout is too far to the right for a reliable entry.

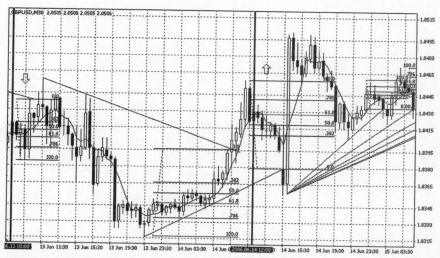

FIGURE 10.10 Crossover Entries and Targets June 13–14
Source: Copyright 2001–2007, MetaQuotes Software Corp.

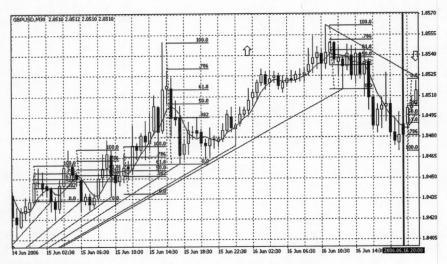

FIGURE 10.11 Crossover Entries and Targets June 15–16
Source: Copyright 2001–2007, MetaQuotes Software Corp.

The fifth trade does not develop fully and reaches the .618 line only before the fall.

The first two trade entries in Figure 10.12 paid very well, while the third one retraced significantly before reaching the target.

Figure 10.13 shows four trade entries upward, the first three of which reached their .618 targets resulting in over 50 pips profit. The fourth trade did not pay, but suffered a 50-pip loss. After the fourth trade the market reversed direction, as we shall see on the next figure.

The first formation in Figure 10.14 did not pay before the second one formed. The procedure that I follow, as you know by now, is to enter the second with more lots and to use the target for the second as the target for both entries. In this case the profit was made with no difficulties.

Figure 10.15 is a busy-looking chart with lines going everywhere. The first trade entry is immediately following the change in direction, as dictated by the four-hour chart, and there is a retracement prior to the movement upward. The chart shows the breakout above the previous high that also paid for us.

The second trade entry did not work so well with a retracement that was large, but not uncalled for. If you entered here, you would know that a large stop-loss value would be required.

In each of the last three trades upward, I would scale back the expectations for profits because of the retracements and use the .50 lines as the targets.

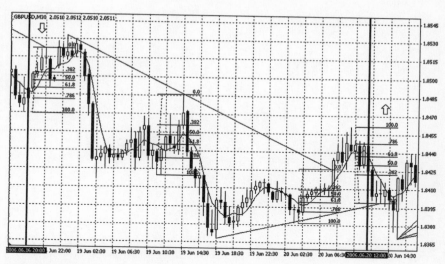

FIGURE 10.12 Crossover Entries and Targets June 19–20
Source: Copyright 2001–2007, MetaQuotes Software Corp.

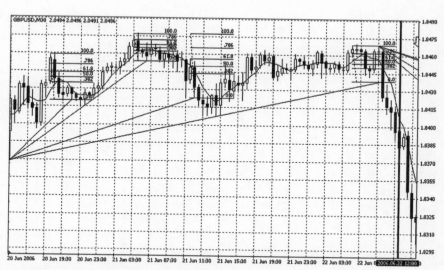

FIGURE 10.13 Crossover Entries and Targets June 20–21
Source: Copyright 2001–2007, MetaQuotes Software Corp.

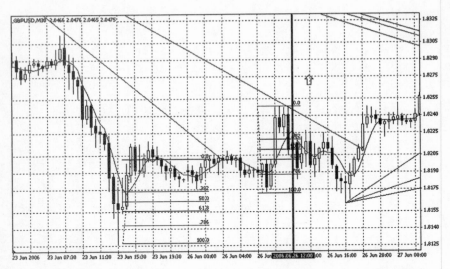

FIGURE 10.14 Crossover Entries and Targets June 23–26
Source: Copyright 2001–2007, MetaQuotes Software Corp.

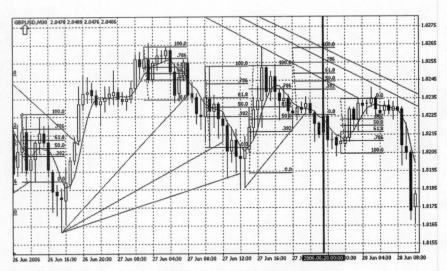

FIGURE 10.15 Crossover Entries and Targets June 26–27
Source: Copyright 2001–2007, MetaQuotes Software Corp.

The bold vertical line represents, of course, the shift in direction to downward trades.

Figure 10.16 shows the market dropping downward with spikes up to the trend lines, which could also be described as "inner trend walls." The first two worked very well, but the last was overridden by the economic announcement. The last trade would be a loser, and I would be reluctant to trade the breakout above the previous resistant point during this announcement because of the uncertainties of these events.

I am not afraid to enter prior to an announcement, but sometimes they do not work, and that is OK with me because of the high success rate overall.

We wrap up June with the two final trades upward as shown in Figure 10.17, the first of which is a very nice bounce off the trend line followed by a breakout. The second is not much, and when you look at the formation you can see that it is very shallow to begin with. There was a similar wide and shallow entry on Figure 10.6, and you can see that in both cases it marked the top of the market move. Because of the retracement while it is developing, I would trade to the .50 line and look for and receive about 10 pips. If I had other interests in movement upward, I would change my plans for the expected downward move that is developing. If I had other trades working that called for U.S dollar weakness, I would become very cautious as this chart is telling us that it is likely to go down, and it could very well be the dollar strength and not the British pound weakness at work here.

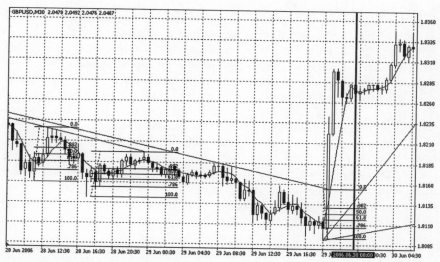

FIGURE 10.16 Crossover Entries and Targets June 28–29
Source: Copyright 2001–2007, MetaQuotes Software Corp.

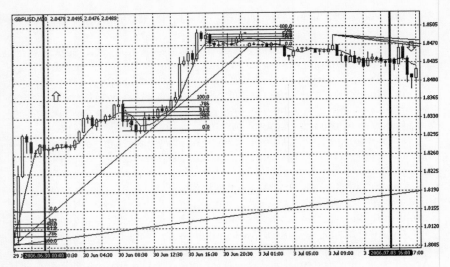

FIGURE 10.17 Crossover Entries and Targets June 30–July 2
Source: Copyright 2001–2007, MetaQuotes Software Corp.

The month of June contains 42 trade entry opportunities, most of which are easy and profitable. The targets are easy to calculate, and the stop-loss values are simple to establish prior to deciding about the entry. I like these trades.

In Figure 10.18 all four entry points worked, although some did retrace first. Looking at the date reminds me that two of those trades are on the Fourth of July, and who said that the market was flat on holidays?

There is a beautiful breakout in Figure 10.19 that I have highlighted with an arrow. Notice how the breakout is in the direction specified by the four-hour chart. Remember that a breakout is where a new low or high is made within about a dozen or fewer candles and the previous low/high, low in this case, was a support or resistance point. In this case it is the ninth candle that broke below the previous low. From this point forward I am going to point out some more of these breakouts because they are a large part of my trading.

To the right there is only one other trade entry going in the same direction before a reversal occurs.

Figure 10.20 covers one complete day with only two trade entries up using this technique. They both did perform as expected, however, one was quite shallow with a small profit.

To the left of the vertical line in Figure 10.21 we have the last entry up from the previous section, and it retraced before reaching the target.

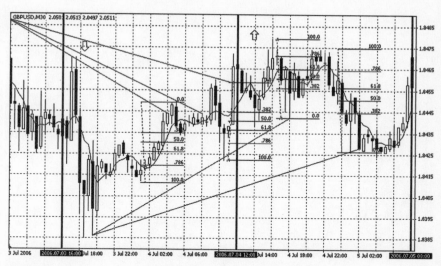

FIGURE 10.18 Crossover Entries and Targets July 3–4
Source: Copyright 2001–2007, MetaQuotes Software Corp.

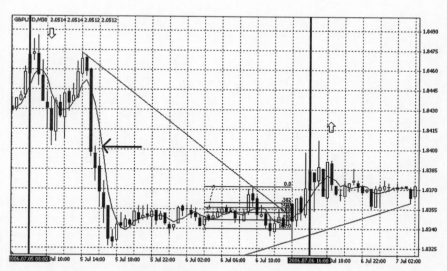

FIGURE 10.19 Crossover Entries and Targets July 5–6
Source: Copyright 2001–2007, MetaQuotes Software Corp.

FIGURE 10.20 Crossover Entries and Targets July 6–7
Source: Copyright 2001–2007, MetaQuotes Software Corp.

FIGURE 10.21 Crossover Entries and Targets July 10–11
Source: Copyright 2001–2007, MetaQuotes Software Corp.

To its right there are two entries down that developed and reached the targets.

The patterns in Figure 10.22 show just one trade entry for the upward section and one for the downward, both of which met their targets.

The leftmost entry in Figure 10.23 shows the last trade down from the previous section, and it did not reach the .618 target.

The first line in the upward section was so shallow that there was not sufficient room for a decent risk-reward ratio, so I did not draw the Fibonacci lines.

The next two overlap, and the second is about as good as it gets.

Notice to the right of each vertical line is a breakout going with the direction of the arrow. Once again, I want to make sure that you are aware of these trading opportunities as they present themselves repeatedly, so I drew two bold black arrows showing where I enter. The stop-loss value for these is about 20 pips above the previous resistance/support point to the left.

Figure 10.24 shows an entry down that did not pay, but because of the excessive retracement after the entry point, I would adjust the target accordingly to help avoid a loss.

The upward section contains just two trades, both of which are successful formations.

The first trade shown in Figure 10.25 was not a good one, but the breakout that I pointed to with an arrow did very well. In this instance,

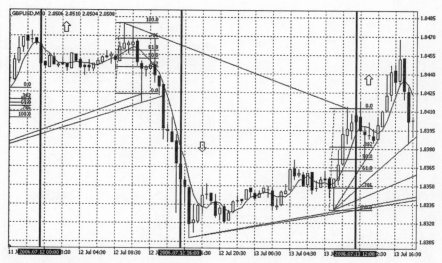

FIGURE 10.22 Crossover Entries and Targets July 12–13
Source: Copyright 2001–2007, MetaQuotes Software Corp.

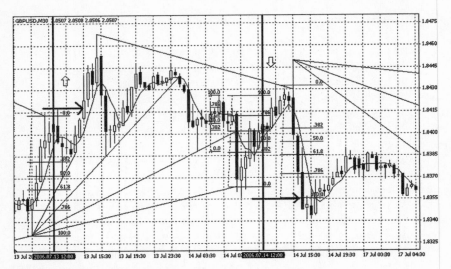

FIGURE 10.23 Crossover Entries and Targets July 13–14
Source: Copyright 2001–2007, MetaQuotes Software Corp.

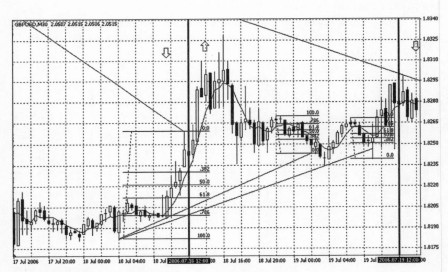

FIGURE 10.24 Crossover Entries and Targets July 17–18
Source: Copyright 2001–2007, MetaQuotes Software Corp.

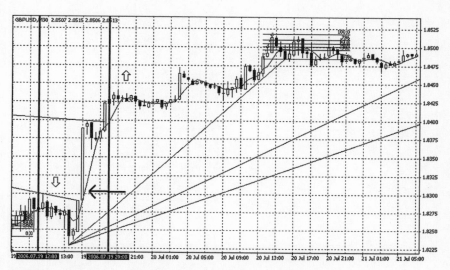

FIGURE 10.25 Crossover Entries and Targets July 19–20
Source: Copyright 2001–2007, MetaQuotes Software Corp.

the announcement was major, and the market moved accordingly. Yes, I will trade a breakout here and have found them to be very profitable.

At the top of the move, there was a slight retracement giving us an opportunity to enter a trade in the direction of the trend.

Figure 10.26 shows an initial loser followed by three beautiful trades. It's like the bankers are saying they are sorry that we lost on that last trade and want to make it up to us. Thank you very much.

Figure 10.27 contains three formations showing the power of this trading technique. Yes, we must always be prepared for retracements prior to the target being reached, but when you see this substantial compilation of evidence, it is reassuring and educational for future reference.

Do you see the breakout down just after the first trade closes?

Figure 10.28 shows four entry opportunities, all of which were quite successful. I did not draw the Fibonacci lines for the second one, but you can see where the market did come back to hit the target.

Figure 10.29 shows the final entries for the month of July, and they were all successful.

If, during the first few days of August, you were looking for an entry into the market going down, you would have needed to wait for the large move up to finally level off, as shown in Figure 10.30.

The large move up caused the four-hour trend to turn, and then these two support points developed for small trades upward with the new trend that was short-lived, as shown in Figure 10.31.

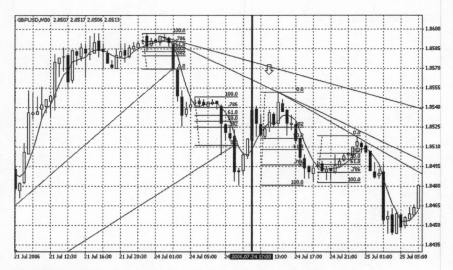

FIGURE 10.26 Crossover Entries and Targets July 21-24
Source: Copyright 2001-2007, MetaQuotes Software Corp.

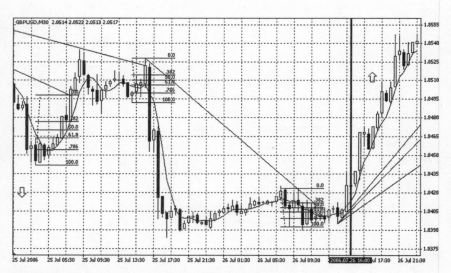

FIGURE 10.27 Crossover Entries and Targets July 25-26
Source: Copyright 2001-2007, MetaQuotes Software Corp.

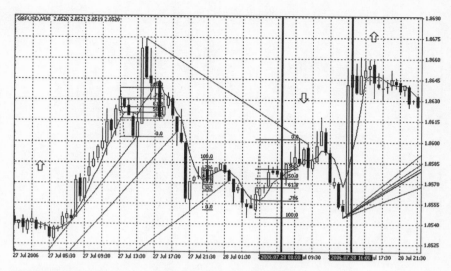

FIGURE 10.28 Crossover Entries and Targets July 27–28
Source: Copyright 2001–2007, MetaQuotes Software Corp.

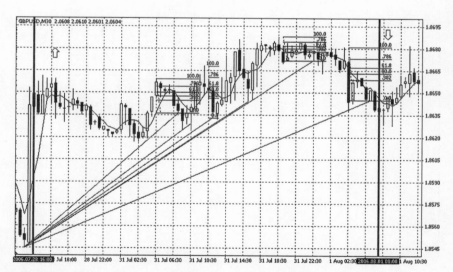

FIGURE 10.29 Crossover Entries and Targets July 28–31
Source: Copyright 2001–2007, MetaQuotes Software Corp.

FIGURE 10.30 Crossover Entries and Targets August 1–2
Source: Copyright 2001–2007, MetaQuotes Software Corp.

FIGURE 10.31 Crossover Entries and Targets August 4–7
Source: Copyright 2001–2007, MetaQuotes Software Corp.

Figure 10.32 shows how volatile the Forex can be as the market moved just enough to change the moving average line direction on the four-hour chart.

The leftmost trade entry down was small and did not pay until the large spike occurred. The second trade paid before the large surge upward.

The entry up to the right is interesting to study because of its large target that was successfully met.

August 9 contains just one trade entry as shown in Figure 10.33. You can see how the .618 target was reached just before the large move downward developed.

The market was unsure what to do following those bold moves, and on August 10 it was range bound and offered us some very good trade entries down, as you can see in Figure 10.34.

Each of the three trades met their targets easily.

Figure 10.35 shows three more formations that developed and were successful before the market changed direction.

Figure 10.36 shows two entry opportunities that were both linked to large moves. These were very nice-looking trades and really help to build the trader's confidence.

Figure 10.37 shows three more successful entries down on August 18 as the market fell.

Figure 10.38 contains just one trade entry that I have shown.

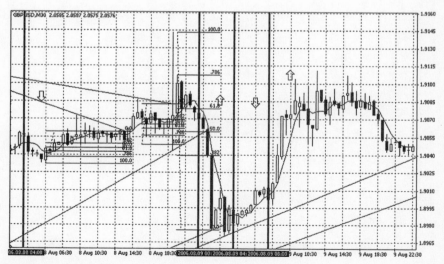

FIGURE 10.32 Crossover Entries and Targets August 8–9
Source: Copyright 2001–2007, MetaQuotes Software Corp.

FIGURE 10.33 Crossover Entries and Targets August 9–10
Source: Copyright 2001–2007, MetaQuotes Software Corp.

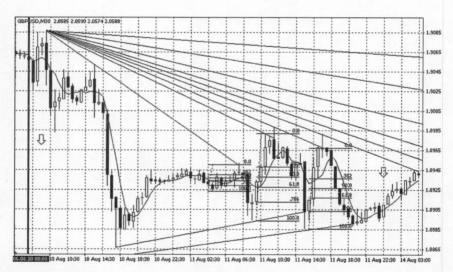

FIGURE 10.34 Crossover Entries and Targets August 10–11
Source: Copyright 2001–2007, MetaQuotes Software Corp.

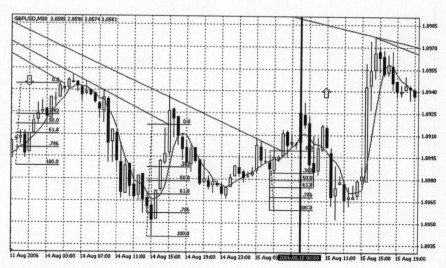

FIGURE 10.35 Crossover Entries and Targets August 14–15
Source: Copyright 2001–2007, MetaQuotes Software Corp.

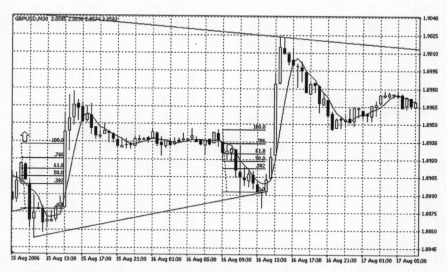

FIGURE 10.36 Crossover Entries and Targets August 15–16
Source: Copyright 2001–2007, MetaQuotes Software Corp.

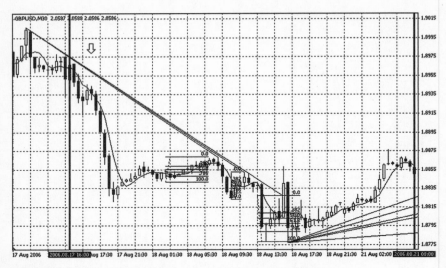

FIGURE 10.37 Crossover Entries and Targets August 17–18
Source: Copyright 2001–2007, MetaQuotes Software Corp.

FIGURE 10.38 Crossover Entries and Targets August 21–22
Source: Copyright 2001–2007, MetaQuotes Software Corp.

But, have you noticed the breakouts? I have not drawn an arrow to it, but there is one to the right of the first vertical bold line. You might want to go back through the previous chart examples and look for these breakouts that I have not already brought to your attention. Remember that I trade them only when they are in the correct direction.

The first trade entry down shown in Figure 10.39 is not a good one. I think that the market must have considered the previous spike that came close to it earlier as the fulfillment, so the market did not honor the one that I have marked.

The second entry up worked well, as can be seen in Figure 10.40.

The entry in Figure 10.40 shows one trade entry up and two down, all of which were good.

Figure 10.41 shows two formations that worked well. The second was another one of those large moves that is very exciting to trade.

The first entry shown in Figure 10.42 is not good, which is very painful following the previous good ones.

The next two entries met their respective targets with one large retracement.

The first trade entry in Figure 10.43 is the same as we discussed in the previous figure, and I wanted to make sure that you could see the large retracement that did not exceed the support point that generated the trend line. This is a large retracement, and it should drive the point home about the need to evaluate the risk before entering any trade.

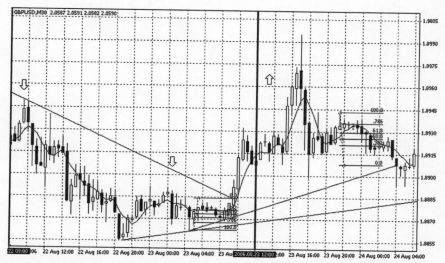

FIGURE 10.39 Crossover Entries and Targets August 22–23
Source: Copyright 2001–2007, MetaQuotes Software Corp.

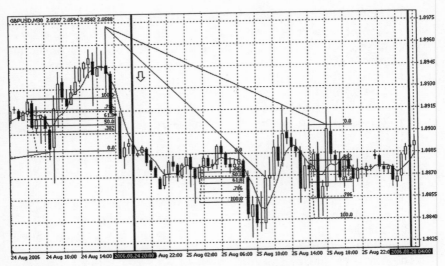

FIGURE 10.40 Crossover Entries and Targets August 24–25
Source: Copyright 2001–2007, MetaQuotes Software Corp.

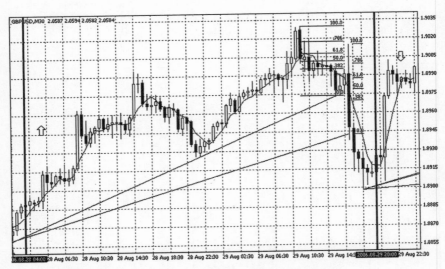

FIGURE 10.41 Crossover Entries and Targets August 28–29
Source: Copyright 2001–2007, MetaQuotes Software Corp.

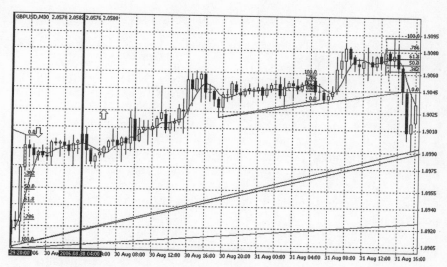

FIGURE 10.42 Crossover Entries and Targets August 30–31
Source: Copyright 2001–2007, MetaQuotes Software Corp.

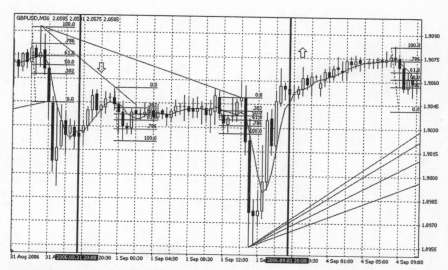

FIGURE 10.43 Crossover Entries and Targets August 31–September 4
Source: Copyright 2001–2007, MetaQuotes Software Corp.

The next two trade entries in the downward section developed and paid well.

Figure 10.44 shows just one trade entry up for that section, and it met its target with no difficulty.

There is another opportunity that I want to discuss at this point. To the right of the second vertical line are three additional trend lines drawn against the trend in that section. They are going up while the trend is going down. What I would like for you to observe is how these trend lines can be used to predict breakout points. For example, notice the end of line A is a potential entry point just like any other you have been studying, except that instead of expecting the market to bounce, you can anticipate additional movement with the trend. I have highlighted three points A, B, and C for you to study. Remember that each line has an inception, pivot, and target.

I suggest that you take the time to go back through this chapter and review other charts to identify these types of opportunities as they presented themselves. The stop-loss value is always a large consideration for any trade, and you will discover how to evaluate this depending upon your risk awareness and tolerance. I will not be drawing these lines on the subsequent charts because they will become too cluttered with excessive lines.

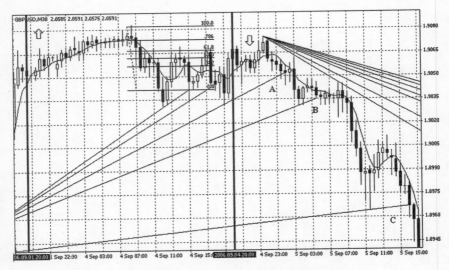

FIGURE 10.44 Crossover Entries and Targets September 4–5
Source: Copyright 2001–2007, MetaQuotes Software Corp.

What I have just described is a very big deal, and it will make a major impact upon your trading and overall success.

The three entries shown in Figure 10.45 were all successful. There are additional breakout opportunities along the way, but they are not easily seen without more history showing to the left.

September 12 had no support points to trade, so maybe this is another good time to show the breakout trend line intersection points. Figure 10.46 shows these lines, and notice how dramatic they are. The stop-loss value can be easily calculated with the Fibonacci drawing tool. Don't be confused now as these lines, when they are hit, are for trading up with the trend.

Both of the down entries shown in Figure 10.47 are successful.

There so many lines in Figure 10.48 that I did not draw all of the targets, but by now you understand how it is done, right?

Figure 10.49 shows three entry points that were all successful.

Why not show you more breakout trend lines? Not much else happening in Figure 10.50, so here we go with breakouts for trading down. See why I like trend lines?

As we wrap up September with Figure 10.51, I have drawn all the lines with no targets. Now, how can we not make profit on days like this? Remember that the top lines are bounces, while the lower lines are breakouts as the trend is still going down.

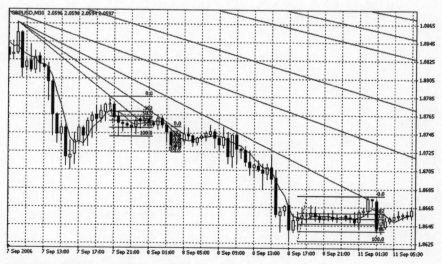

FIGURE 10.45 Crossover Entries and Targets September 7–8
Source: Copyright 2001–2007, MetaQuotes Software Corp.

FIGURE 10.46 Crossover Entries and Targets September 12–13
Source: Copyright 2001–2007, MetaQuotes Software Corp.

FIGURE 10.47 Crossover Entries and Targets September 15–18
Source: Copyright 2001–2007, MetaQuotes Software Corp.

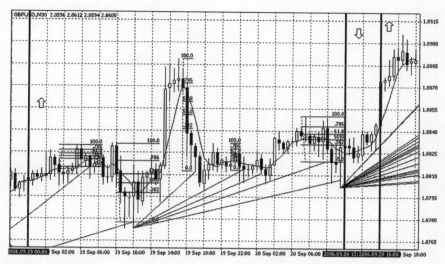

FIGURE 10.48 Crossover Entries and Targets September 19–20
Source: Copyright 2001–2007, MetaQuotes Software Corp.

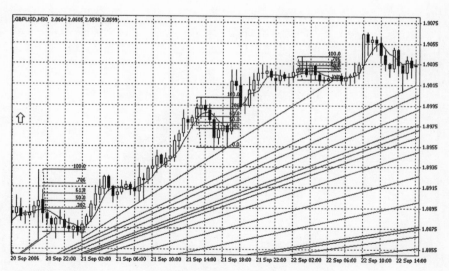

FIGURE 10.49 Crossover Entries and Targets September 20–21
Source: Copyright 2001–2007, MetaQuotes Software Corp.

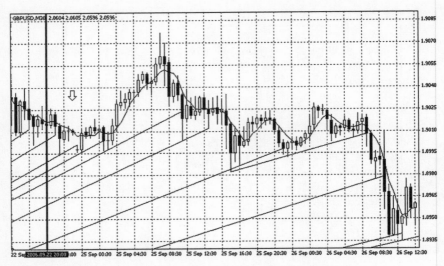

FIGURE 10.50 Crossover Entries and Targets September 22–25
Source: Copyright 2001–2007, MetaQuotes Software Corp.

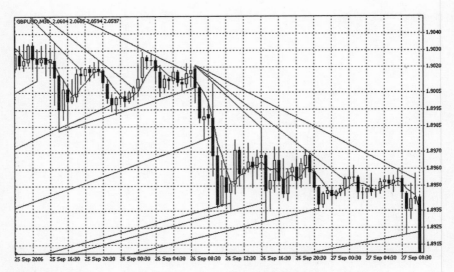

FIGURE 10.51 Crossover Entries and Targets September 25–26
Source: Copyright 2001–2007, MetaQuotes Software Corp.

SUMMARY

This study is the most exciting because the combination of trend lines and Fibonacci lines is the most powerful. The trend lines identify the key decision points for the market. They help us to always be current and looking in the right direction. Using the four-hour chart for the direction does have its weak moments when the market is indecisive, but over the long haul, as we say, it serves very well.

If you missed the figures that describe the trend line-related breakouts, please go back and review them beginning with Figure 10.44, because this is as much as 50 percent of the trading opportunities using these tools. It is almost unbelievable how many entries are presented for the trader when one knows what to look for.

Trend lines help us to trade the "bounce" with the trend and the "breakout" with the trend over and over again.

Loss Recovery in Practice

I t is easy to write a book about how to trade, but it is quite another to put the rules into practice and let the market decide whether or not it works. So, as I am completing this manuscript it seems appropriate to include a report showing the results of these rules that I have set before you for your consideration.

Figure 11.1 is a copy of the broker report for a small mini account that I have been trading for your benefit and mine for the last two weeks. It contains many trades that I have entered manually, and it contains many trades that I monitored as I worked full time developing several trading robots. As you can see, the report begins with the account activity on October 12, 2007, and ends November 1, 2007. There are 27 losing trades out of 147 total trades. The net profit was $5,140.18, representing a gain of 187 percent for the 20-day period.

The report shows some very good trades and some mistakes, and there are some trades entered with very poor judgment. Just yesterday I referenced a demo account for the four-hour trend and it was not accurate, so I entered in the wrong direction. Brokers use different servers for demo and real accounts, and the resulting differences in data often cause a variation in oscillator and moving average values. Yesterday, these differences affected my trading outcome. But, when the trading system is reliable it is not discouraging or debilitating. When mistakes are made, it is easy to wipe off the dirt, so to speak, and get back to work.

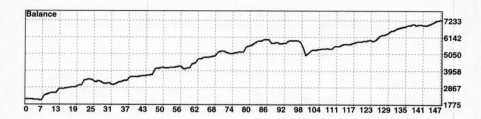

Account: 24357 **Name:** Gerald Greene **Currency:** USD 2007 November 1, 14:06

Closed Transactions:

Ticket	Open Time	Type	Size	Item	Price	S / L	T / P	Close Time	Price	Commission	Taxes	Swap	Profit
21326107	2007.11.01 13:59	sell	4.00	eurusdm	1.4420	0.0000	1.4391	2007.11.01 14:04	1.4408	0.00	0.00	0.00	48.00
												Trend line Breakout	
21323980	2007.11.01 13:05	buy limit	4.00	usdjpym	114.80	114.21	115.00	2007.11.01 13:58	114.93				cancelled
21323062	2007.11.01 12:52	sell	4.00	usdcadm	0.9463	0.9545	0.0000	2007.11.01 12:58	0.9458	0.00	0.00	0.00	21.15
												Trend line Bounce	
21317649	2007.11.01 11:02	sell	4.00	usdcadm	0.9458	0.9552	0.9425	2007.11.01 12:03	0.9442	0.00	0.00	0.00	67.78
												Trend line Bounce	
21317204	2007.11.01 10:26	sell	8.00	usdcadm	0.9440	0.9520	0.9415	2007.11.01 12:13	0.9429	0.00	0.00	0.00	93.33
												Trend line Breakout	
21316484	2007.11.01 09:32	sell	8.00	eurjpym	166.85	167.31	166.66	2007.11.01 12:37	166.69	0.00	0.00	0.00	110.78
												X	
21316131	2007.11.01 09:16	buy	2.00	gbpjpym	240.49	239.11	242.12	2007.11.01 10:07	240.34	0.00	0.00	0.00	-25.93
									16384			FR022	
21314864	2007.11.01 08:30	buy	2.00	gbpjpym	240.51	239.11	242.11	2007.11.01 10:07	240.33	0.00	0.00	0.00	-31.12
									16384			FR021	
21312115	2007.11.01 07:17	buy	8.00	gbpjpym	240.28	239.11	242.11	2007.11.01 10:07	240.33	0.00	0.00	0.00	34.57
												X	
21312058	2007.11.01 07:14	buy	4.00	eurjpym	166.99	0.00	0.00	2007.11.01 07:30	167.14	0.00	0.00	0.00	51.94
												X	
21306568	2007.11.01 01:08	sell	4.00	gbpjpym	239.94	240.31	238.94	2007.11.01 07:17	240.20	0.00	0.00	0.00	-90.07
												X	
21297129	2007.10.31 18:25	sell	2.00	usdcadm	0.9521	0.9585	0.9499	2007.10.31 18:31	0.9499	0.00	0.00	0.00	46.32
												Trend Line Bounce[tp]	
21291388	2007.10.31 15:27	buy limit	4.00	gbpusdm	2.0704	2.0657	2.0715	2007.10.31 16:16	2.0780				cancelled
21291125	2007.10.31 14:52	sell	4.00	usdcadm	0.9504	0.9578	0.9489	2007.10.31 18:33	0.9489	0.00	0.00	0.00	63.23

FIGURE 11.1 Interbank FX, LLC

Ticket	Open Time	Type	Size	Item	Price	S/L	T/P	Close Time	Price				Profit
												Breakout[tp]	
21288491	2007.10.31 12:38	buy	4.00	gbpusdm	2.0703	2.0541	2.0725	2007.10.31 13:08	2.0718	0.00	0.00	0.00	60.00
												Trend line Bounce	
21287495	2007.10.31 12:17	buy	4.00	usdjpym	115.30	114.27	115.42	2007.10.31 14:27	115.42	0.00	0.00	0.00	41.59
												Trend line Breakout[tp]	
21286325	2007.10.31 10:48	buy limit	4.00	gbpusdm	2.0707	0.0000	2.0725	2007.10.31 11:24	2.0727				cancelled
21285050	2007.10.31 09:53	buy	4.00	eurusdm	1.4434	1.4374	1.4452	2007.10.31 10:26	1.4452	0.00	0.00	0.00	72.00
												Trend line Bounce[tp]	
21284824	2007.10.31 09:36	buy	4.00	eurusdm	1.4443	1.4380	1.4452	2007.10.31 10:26	1.4452	0.00	0.00	0.00	36.00
												Trend line Bounce[tp]	
21283408	2007.10.31 08:26	buy	2.00	gbpjpym	238.32	236.53	239.68	2007.10.31 10:03	238.73	0.00	0.00	0.00	71.22
					16384							FR024	
21283401	2007.10.31 08:26	buy	2.00	gbpjpym	238.36	236.53	239.67	2007.10.31 10:03	238.73	0.00	0.00	0.00	64.27
					16384							FR023	
21282400	2007.10.31 07:31	buy	2.00	gbpjpym	238.03	238.23	239.66	2007.10.31 10:03	238.72	0.00	0.00	0.00	119.86
					16384							FR022	
21282397	2007.10.31 07:31	buy	2.00	gbpjpym	238.05	238.25	239.65	2007.10.31 10:03	238.72	0.00	0.00	0.00	116.39
					16384							FR021	
21276228	2007.10.30 23:57	buy	4.00	gbpjpym	237.35	236.74	237.85	2007.10.31 07:15	237.85	0.00	0.00	0.00	174.36
												X[tp]	
21276225	2007.10.30 23:56	buy	4.00	gbpjpym	237.35	236.75	237.85	2007.10.31 07:15	237.85	0.00	0.00	0.00	174.36
												X[tp]	
21275750	2007.10.30 22:30	buy	4.00	gbpjpym	237.20	0.00	237.27	2007.10.30 23:18	237.27	0.00	0.00	0.00	24.41
												Trend line Bounce[tp]	
21274165	2007.10.30 20:08	sell	4.00	gbpjpym	237.18	237.80	235.98	2007.10.30 23:57	237.35	0.00	0.00	-13.49	-59.26
												X	
21273177	2007.10.30 19:33	buy	4.00	usdjpym	114.73	114.31	114.88	2007.10.31 08:05	114.88	0.00	0.00	4.76	52.23
												Trend line Bounce[tp]	
21269494	2007.10.30 15:26	sell	4.00	usdcadm	0.9537	0.9594	0.9525	2007.10.30 17:56	0.9532	0.00	0.00	0.00	20.98
												Breakout	

FIGURE 11.1 Interbank FX, LLC (*Cont.*)

21265988	2007.10.30 14:00	sell	4.00	usdcadm	0.9543	0.9594	0.9528	2007.10.30 17:56	0.9531	0.00	0.00	0.00	50.36
												Trend line Breakout	
21265046	2007.10.30 12:36	buy	4.00	usdjpym	114.89	114.31	115.05	2007.10.31 08:26	114.93	0.00	0.00	4.76	13.92
												Trend line Breakout	
21262137	2007.10.30 09:27	sell	2.00	usdjpym	114.65	0.00	0.00	2007.10.30 12:36	114.89	0.00	0.00	0.00	-41.78
												Trend line Bounce	
21261237	2007.10.30 08:53	buy	2.00	gbpjpym	236.95	235.04	237.45	2007.10.30 15:45	237.01	0.00	0.00	0.00	10.47
									16384			FR024	
21261216	2007.10.30 08:53	buy	2.00	gbpjpym	236.93	235.04	237.43	2007.10.30 15:45	236.99	0.00	0.00	0.00	10.47
									16384			FR023	
21260721	2007.10.30 08:44	buy	2.00	gbpjpym	236.61	235.04	237.41	2007.10.30 15:45	237.00	0.00	0.00	0.00	68.03
									16384			FR022	
21260708	2007.10.30 08:44	buy	2.00	gbpjpym	236.64	235.04	237.44	2007.10.30 15:45	237.00	0.00	0.00	0.00	62.81
									16384			FR021	
21260427	2007.10.30 08:17	buy	4.00	eurjpym	165.11	0.00	0.00	2007.10.30 08:47	165.30	0.00	0.00	0.00	66.27
												River X	
21259737	2007.10.30 07:54	buy	4.00	gbpusdm	2.0621	0.0000	0.0000	2007.10.30 08:46	2.0639	0.00	0.00	0.00	72.00
												Trend line Breakout	
21253461	2007.10.30 01:39	buy stop	4.00	gbpjpym	236.85	234.96	237.27	2007.10.30 08:11	236.43				cancelled
21250643	2007.10.29 23:28	sell	4.00	eurjpym	165.29	165.53	164.35	2007.10.30 01:13	164.77	0.00	0.00	0.00	181.66
												X	
21249562	2007.10.29 21:14	buy	2.00	eurjpym	165.49	164.90	165.69	2007.10.29 23:29	165.30	0.00	0.00	0.00	-33.14
												Trend line Breakout	
21247944	2007.10.29 18:41	sell	2.00	eurusdm	1.4422	1.4442	1.4358	2007.10.30 13:26	1.4408	0.00	0.00	0.56	28.00
												TYPE1	
21247931	2007.10.29 18:40	sell	2.00	eurusdm	1.4420	0.0000	0.0000	2007.10.29 18:41	1.4423	0.00	0.00	0.00	-6.00
												TYPE1	
21247711	2007.10.29 18:16	sell	1.00	gbpjpym	236.37	236.35	234.45	2007.10.30 07:49	235.90	0.00	0.00	-3.37	41.05
												XPrelim	
21247623	2007.10.29 18:02	buy stop	2.00	eurjpym	165.53	0.00	165.68	2007.10.29 21:13	165.46				cancelled

FIGURE 11.1 Interbank FX, LLC (*Cont.*)

21246232	2007.10.29 15:59	buy	2.00	gbpjpym	236.44	235.75	236.55	2007.10.29 16:09	236.55	0.00	0.00	0.00	19.18
											Trend line Breakout[tp]		
21244163	2007.10.29 14:08	buy	2.00	gbpusdm	2.0577	2.0578	2.0600	2007.10.29 15:07	2.0600	0.00	0.00	0.00	46.00
											Fib[tp]		
21243890	2007.10.29 14:00	sell	3.00	usdcadm	0.9608	0.0000	0.9601	2007.10.29 14:29	0.9601	0.00	0.00	0.00	21.87
											Fib[tp]		
21240333	2007.10.29 11:39	sell	1.00	gbpjpym	236.64	236.63	234.39	2007.10.29 13:46	236.63	0.00	0.00	0.00	0.87
											XPrelim[sl]		
21240027	2007.10.29 11:33	buy	2.00	eurusdm	1.4414	1.4339	1.4427	2007.10.29 17:10	1.4423	0.00	0.00	0.00	18.00
											Fib		
21239186	2007.10.29 11:09	sell	1.00	gbpjpym	235.98	236.85	234.39	2007.10.30 07:49	235.90	0.00	0.00	-3.37	6.99
											XProvisional		
21237513	2007.10.29 10:08	buy	4.00	gbpjpym	235.30	235.58	235.89	2007.10.29 10:54	235.76	0.00	0.00	0.00	160.72
											Breakout		
21227157	2007.10.26 18:45	buy	4.00	gbpjpym	234.56	233.56	235.46	2007.10.29 07:00	235.08	0.00	0.00	11.00	182.02
											River X		
21226652	2007.10.26 17:17	sell	4.00	gbpusdm	2.0505	2.0577	2.0465	2007.10.29 06:46	2.0577	0.00	0.00	-1.98	-288.00
											Fib[sl]		
21225845	2007.10.26 16:04	sell	8.00	gbpusdm	2.0503	2.0577	2.0465	2007.10.29 06:46	2.0577	0.00	0.00	-3.96	-592.00
											[sl]		
21224900	2007.10.26 14:48	sell	4.00	gbpjpym	234.19	0.00	233.42	2007.10.26 16:01	233.85	0.00	0.00	0.00	119.28
											FR021		
21223859	2007.10.26 13:58	sell stop	5.00	gbpusdm	2.0478	0.0000	2.0458	2007.10.26 17:04	2.0507				cancelled
21223675	2007.10.26 13:40	sell	3.00	usdcadm	0.9633	0.9632	0.9609	2007.10.26 15:17	0.9615	0.00	0.00	0.00	56.16
											Trend line		
21222881	2007.10.26 12:51	buy	3.00	usdjpym	114.41	0.00	114.45	2007.10.26 13:33	114.45	0.00	0.00	0.00	10.48
											Trend line[tp]		
21221252	2007.10.26 11:44	sell	5.00	eurusdm	1.4365	1.4383	1.4345	2007.10.26 12:14	1.4383	0.00	0.00	0.00	-90.00
											Reversal[sl]		
21220507	2007.10.26 10:55	buy	2.00	gbpusdm	2.0515	2.0451	2.0550	2007.10.26 19:09	2.0520	0.00	0.00	0.00	10.00

FIGURE 11.1 Interbank FX, LLC (*Cont.*)

											Trend line		
21219866	2007.10.26 10:34	buy	1.00	gbpusdm	2.0521	2.0451	2.0550	2007.10.26 19:11	2.0522	0.00	0.00	0.00	1.00
											Trend line		
21219507	2007.10.26 10:24	buy	1.00	gbpusdm	2.0530	2.0451	2.0561	2007.10.28 22:21	2.0545	0.00	0.00	0.48	15.00
											Trend line		
21219255	2007.10.26 10:02	buy	3.00	gbpjpym	234.74	0.00	234.94	2007.10.26 10:10	234.94	0.00	0.00	0.00	52.44
											Trend line[tp]		
21218028	2007.10.26 08:29	buy	3.00	gbpusdm	2.0566	2.0479	2.0571	2007.10.29 00:46	2.0530	0.00	0.00	1.43	-108.00
											Breakout		
21217750	2007.10.26 08:12	sell	3.00	usdcadm	0.9617	0.9715	0.9600	2007.10.26 08:49	0.9614	0.00	0.00	0.00	9.36
											Breakout		
21207234	2007.10.25 19:00	buy	5.00	eurusdm	1.4321	1.4267	1.4333	2007.10.25 20:38	1.4322	0.00	0.00	0.00	5.00
											Hedge		
21206206	2007.10.25 17:52	sell	2.00	eurusdm	1.4321	1.4349	1.4301	2007.10.25 19:01	1.4320	0.00	0.00	0.00	2.00
											Cost Average		
21205232	2007.10.25 17:14	sell	3.00	eurusdm	1.4298	1.4375	1.4235	2007.10.26 06:38	1.4375	0.00	0.00	0.84	-231.00
											TYPE1[sl]		
21203134	2007.10.25 15:14	buy	3.00	gbpjpym	233.92	232.69	234.23	2007.10.25 15:34	234.23	0.00	0.00	0.00	81.39
											Trend line[tp]		
21200786	2007.10.25 13:40	buy	2.00	gbpjpym	233.95	233.31	234.55	2007.10.25 14:11	234.55	0.00	0.00	0.00	104.97
											Cost Avg[tp]		
21198232	2007.10.25 12:42	buy	2.00	gbpjpym	234.58	233.31	234.77	2007.10.25 14:11	234.59	0.00	0.00	0.00	1.75
											Cost Avg		
21194790	2007.10.25 10:39	buy	2.00	gbpjpym	234.45	233.96	0.00	2007.10.25 11:23	234.87	0.00	0.00	0.00	73.36
											Cost Avg		
21194328	2007.10.25 10:26	buy	2.00	gbpjpym	234.76	233.96	237.51	2007.10.25 11:22	234.91	0.00	0.00	0.00	26.20
								16384				FR024		
21191652	2007.10.25 08:29	buy	4.00	gbpjpym	233.99	234.03	235.09	2007.10.25 11:23	234.87	0.00	0.00	0.00	307.43
								16384				FR021		
21191327	2007.10.25 08:16	buy	2.00	gbpjpym	234.28	0.00	234.69	2007.10.25 10:02	234.35	0.00	0.00	0.00	12.25

FIGURE 11.1   Interbank FX, LLC (*Cont.*)

												Retracement	
21191216	2007.10.25 08:11	buy	2.00	gbpjpym	234.45	233.99	235.05	2007.10.25 11:23	234.88	0.00	0.00	0.00	75.10
									16384			FR023	
21190809	2007.10.25 07:57	buy	2.00	gbpjpym	233.93	0.00	234.33	2007.10.25 08:11	234.33	0.00	0.00	0.00	69.95
												Retracement[tp]	
21190113	2007.10.25 07:07	buy	2.00	gbpjpym	234.06	234.12	235.06	2007.10.25 11:23	234.88	0.00	0.00	0.00	143.23
									16384			FR022	
21189902	2007.10.25 07:01	buy	4.00	gbpjpym	233.74	233.83	235.63	2007.10.25 08:29	233.83	0.00	0.00	0.00	31.52
									16384			FR021[sl]	
21187751	2007.10.25 05:15	sell	2.00	gbpjpym	233.09	233.64	230.34	2007.10.25 06:22	233.64	0.00	0.00	0.00	-96.42
									16384			FR023[sl]	
21183919	2007.10.25 01:00	sell	2.00	gbpjpym	233.40	233.71	232.10	2007.10.25 06:30	233.60	0.00	0.00	0.00	-35.07
									16384			FR022	
21183901	2007.10.25 01:00	sell	4.00	gbpjpym	233.40	233.71	232.10	2007.10.25 06:30	233.61	0.00	0.00	0.00	-73.63
									16384			FR021	
21180659	2007.10.24 19:13	sell	1.00	gbpjpym	234.19	234.99	233.85	2007.10.24 19:23	234.03	0.00	0.00	0.00	14.02
												Trend line	
21170257	2007.10.24 13:04	sell	2.00	gbpjpym	234.35	0.00	0.00	2007.10.24 14:02	233.98	0.00	0.00	0.00	64.84
												Trend line	
21169704	2007.10.24 12:50	sell	2.00	eurjpym	162.73	163.37	162.37	2007.10.24 14:12	162.58	0.00	0.00	0.00	26.29
												Trend line	
21168270	2007.10.24 11:45	sell	2.00	gbpjpym	234.19	0.00	233.89	2007.10.24 12:02	234.13	0.00	0.00	0.00	10.49
												Trend line	
21163963	2007.10.24 08:30	sell	2.00	gbpjpym	234.59	0.00	0.00	2007.10.24 11:33	234.09	0.00	0.00	0.00	87.50
												Trend line	
21163356	2007.10.24 08:12	sell	2.00	gbpjpym	233.96	0.00	0.00	2007.10.24 11:36	233.89	0.00	0.00	0.00	12.25
												Fib	
21161157	2007.10.24 07:18	sell	2.00	gbpjpym	233.44	235.83	232.10	2007.10.24 15:19	233.09	0.00	0.00	0.00	61.46
									16384			FR022	
21160456	2007.10.24 07:06	sell	4.00	gbpjpym	233.74	235.83	233.04	2007.10.24 15:18	233.04	0.00	0.00	0.00	245.90

FIGURE 11.1 Interbank FX, LLC (*Cont.*)

							16384				FR021[tp]		
21146912	2007.10.23 15:50	buy	2.00	eurusdm	1.4249	1.4224	1.4262	2007.10.23 19:02	1.4252	0.00	0.00	0.00	6.00
											Fib		
21138640	2007.10.23 11:30	buy	2.00	gbpjpym	234.53	233.16	235.76	2007.10.23 12:27	234.89	0.00	0.00	0.00	62.78
							16384				FR022		
21137697	2007.10.23 11:03	sell	2.00	usdcadm	0.9713	0.9745	0.9703	2007.10.23 11:12	0.9703	0.00	0.00	0.00	20.61
											Breakout[tp]		
21137639	2007.10.23 11:00	buy	6.00	eurjpym	162.91	162.93	163.65	2007.10.23 12:28	163.38	0.00	0.00	0.00	245.91
											X		
21136221	2007.10.23 09:49	buy	4.00	gbpjpym	234.12	234.22	235.76	2007.10.23 12:27	234.88	0.00	0.00	0.00	265.06
							16384				FR021		
21136015	2007.10.23 09:35	buy	2.00	eurjpym	162.55	161.87	162.81	2007.10.23 10:56	162.81	0.00	0.00	0.00	45.39
											Fib[tp]		
21135891	2007.10.23 09:20	sell	4.00	usdcadm	0.9713	0.9747	0.9703	2007.10.23 11:12	0.9703	0.00	0.00	0.00	41.22
											Breakout[tp]		
21133213	2007.10.23 07:48	sell	4.00	eurjpym	162.37	0.00	162.07	2007.10.23 11:00	162.90	0.00	0.00	0.00	-184.98
											X		
21124763	2007.10.23 00:34	buy limit	1.00	eurusdm	1.4155	1.4095	0.0000	2007.10.23 07:57	1.4213				cancelled
21124721	2007.10.23 00:28	buy	1.00	eurusdm	1.4182	1.4085	0.0000	2007.10.23 07:57	1.4212	0.00	0.00	0.00	30.00
											TYPE1		
21121167	2007.10.22 19:49	buy	2.00	usdjpym	114.29	114.11	114.41	2007.10.22 20:35	114.41	0.00	0.00	0.00	20.98
											Fib[tp]		
21115531	2007.10.22 15:19	sell	2.00	eurusdm	1.4137	0.0000	1.4124	2007.10.22 15:48	1.4130	0.00	0.00	0.00	14.00
											Fib		
21113681	2007.10.22 14:46	sell	1.00	eurusdm	1.4164	0.0000	1.4144	2007.10.22 14:49	1.4154	0.00	0.00	0.00	10.00
											Fib		
21105144	2007.10.22 11:38	buy	2.00	eurusdm	1.4188	1.4175	1.4200	2007.10.22 11:42	1.4175	0.00	0.00	0.00	-26.00
											Fib[sl]		
21096443	2007.10.22 09:38	sell	2.00	eurusdm	1.4293	0.0000	1.4283	2007.10.22 09:50	1.4283	0.00	0.00	0.00	20.00
											Trend line Breakout[tp]		

FIGURE 11.1 Interbank FX, LLC (*Cont.*)

21094365	2007.10.22 09:33	sell	2.00	gbpusdm	2.0467	2.0499	2.0447	2007.10.22 09:38	2.0447	0.00	0.00	0.00	40.00
												Trend line[tp]	
21095560	2007.10.22 08:51	sell	2.00	gbpjpym	233.06	0.00	232.61	2007.10.22 09:01	232.78	0.00	0.00	0.00	49.26
												FR021	
21094977	2007.10.22 08:21	buy	2.00	usdcadm	0.9694	0.9635	0.9704	2007.10.22 09:13	0.9704	0.00	0.00	0.00	20.61
												Fib[tp]	
21094396	2007.10.22 07:46	buy stop	6.00	gbpjpym	234.92	0.00	235.13	2007.10.22 08:58	232.89				cancelled
21094244	2007.10.22 07:36	sell	6.00	gbpjpym	233.47	234.74	232.41	2007.10.22 09:01	232.79	0.00	0.00	0.00	358.90
												FR021	
21089211	2007.10.22 03:18	buy	4.00	eurusdm	1.4317	1.4301	1.4327	2007.10.22 05:49	1.4327	0.00	0.00	0.00	40.00
												Fib[tp]	
21078362	2007.10.19 17:36	buy	2.00	gbpusdm	2.0482	2.0431	2.0500	2007.10.19 18:48	2.0500	0.00	0.00	0.00	36.00
												Fib[tp]	
21077409	2007.10.19 15:55	buy	2.00	eurusdm	1.4262	1.4243	1.4274	2007.10.19 18:04	1.4274	0.00	0.00	0.00	24.00
												Fib[tp]	
21077147	2007.10.19 15:46	sell stop	2.00	eurusdm	1.4243	0.0000	0.0000	2007.10.19 17:48	1.4272				cancelled
21072851	2007.10.19 14:03	buy	4.00	eurusdm	1.4273	1.4215	1.4279	2007.10.19 18:11	1.4279	0.00	0.00	0.00	24.00
												Trend line[tp]	
21071542	2007.10.19 12:18	sell	4.00	eurusdm	1.4287	0.0000	1.4165	2007.10.19 18:38	1.4289	0.00	0.00	0.00	-8.00
												Type1	
21069391	2007.10.19 10:12	buy	4.00	gbpjpym	236.32	234.72	236.83	2007.10.19 10:34	236.83	0.00	0.00	0.00	176.36
									16384			FR021[tp]	
21068722	2007.10.19 09:51	sell	4.00	gbpjpym	235.90	238.35	235.34	2007.10.19 14:07	235.83	0.00	0.00	0.00	24.32
												Fib	
21068103	2007.10.19 08:55	buy	2.00	eurusdm	1.4284	1.4165	1.4297	2007.10.19 12:18	1.4287	0.00	0.00	0.00	6.00
												Fib	
21059562	2007.10.19 00:51	buy	2.00	gbpusdm	2.0438	2.0375	2.0475	2007.10.19 03:17	2.0475	0.00	0.00	0.00	74.00
												Trend line[tp]	
21059252	2007.10.19 00:46	buy	2.00	gbpusdm	2.0456	2.0375	2.0475	2007.10.19 03:17	2.0475	0.00	0.00	0.00	38.00
												Trend line[tp]	

FIGURE 11.1 Interbank FX, LLC (*Cont.*)

Ticket	Open Time	Type	Size	Item	Price	S/L	T/P	Close Time	Price				Profit	Comment
21052129	2007.10.18 14:39	sell	4.00	gbpjpym	236.67	237.35	235.99	2007.10.18 15:31	236.57	0.00	0.00	0.00	34.61	FR021
21043057	2007.10.18 08:37	sell	6.00	gbpjpym	237.08	236.88	235.35	2007.10.18 13:08	236.88	0.00	0.00	0.00	103.78	FR021[sl]
21042103	2007.10.18 08:06	buy	2.00	gbpusdm	2.0406	2.0365	2.0417	2007.10.18 08:30	2.0417	0.00	0.00	0.00	22.00	Fib[tp]
21041968	2007.10.18 08:04	sell	4.00	gbpjpym	236.99	237.32	236.09	2007.10.18 08:30	237.32	0.00	0.00	0.00	-113.71	16384 FR021[sl]
21041502	2007.10.18 07:42	buy	2.00	gbpusdm	2.0417	2.0365	2.0423	2007.10.18 08:30	2.0423	0.00	0.00	0.00	12.00	Fib[tp]
21037461	2007.10.18 03:23	buy	4.00	gbpjpym	237.69	235.64	238.59	2007.10.18 03:30	237.55	0.00	0.00	0.00	-48.10	16384 FR021
21029920	2007.10.17 19:47	buy	4.00	gbpjpym	237.70	235.64	238.60	2007.10.17 21:27	237.87	0.00	0.00	33.00	58.29	16384 FR021
21024827	2007.10.17 16:32	buy	4.00	eurjpym	165.48	165.25	165.58	2007.10.17 16:57	165.25	0.00	0.00	0.00	-79.02	Fib[sl]
21022202	2007.10.17 14:55	buy	4.00	eurjpym	165.65	165.24	166.05	2007.10.17 16:58	165.24	0.00	0.00	0.00	-140.86	Trend line[sl]
21018626	2007.10.17 12:37	buy	2.00	eurusdm	1.4201	1.4141	1.4222	2007.10.17 13:33	1.4222	0.00	0.00	0.00	42.00	Hedge[tp]
21017181	2007.10.17 11:56	buy	2.00	eurusdm	1.4187	1.4150	1.4200	2007.10.17 12:15	1.4200	0.00	0.00	0.00	26.00	Trend line[tp]
21013678	2007.10.17 08:42	sell	2.00	eurusdm	1.4176	1.4245	1.4163	2007.10.18 06:52	1.4245	0.00	0.00	1.68	-138.00	Fib[sl]
21012750	2007.10.17 08:12	buy	3.00	eurjpym	165.53	164.22	166.33	2007.10.17 10:45	165.54	0.00	0.00	0.00	2.57	16384 FR0211017
21012334	2007.10.17 07:58	buy	4.00	gbpjpym	237.41	237.61	238.45	2007.10.17 11:27	238.45	0.00	0.00	0.00	355.19	FR021[tp]
21011245	2007.10.17 07:41	buy	2.00	gbpjpym	236.92	235.71	237.42	2007.10.17 07:57	237.42	0.00	0.00	0.00	85.76	Manual[tp]

FIGURE 11.1 Interbank FX, LLC (*Cont.*)

20987257	2007.10.16 08:33	sell	1.00	gbpjpym	238.30	239.31	0.00	2007.10.16 08:45	237.81	0.00	0.00	0.00	41.88
												Manual	
20987163	2007.10.16 08:31	sell	1.00	gbpjpym	238.01	239.29	0.00	2007.10.16 08:45	237.81	0.00	0.00	0.00	17.09
												Manual	
20986372	2007.10.16 08:19	buy	2.00	eurusdm	1.4171	1.4151	0.0000	2007.10.16 08:34	1.4181	0.00	0.00	0.00	20.00
												Fib	
20982918	2007.10.16 07:26	sell	2.00	gbpjpym	238.35	238.25	236.61	2007.10.16 08:12	238.25	0.00	0.00	0.00	17.10
												[sl]	
20982705	2007.10.16 07:24	sell	4.00	gbpjpym	238.16	238.06	236.61	2007.10.16 07:51	238.06	0.00	0.00	0.00	34.21
												[sl]	
20982596	2007.10.16 07:24	sell	4.00	eurjpym	165.96	0.00	165.09	2007.10.16 07:32	165.09	0.00	0.00	0.00	298.48
												[tp]	
20982548	2007.10.16 07:24	sell	4.00	eurjpym	165.96	0.00	164.96	2007.10.16 07:24	166.02	0.00	0.00	0.00	-20.52
												FR021	
20972824	2007.10.15 18:58	buy	1.00	eurusdm	1.4199	1.4163	1.4213	2007.10.15 20:39	1.4209	0.00	0.00	0.00	10.00
												Trend line	
20966600	2007.10.15 14:03	buy	2.00	eurusdm	1.4229	1.4129	1.4269	2007.10.18 10:39	1.4269	0.00	0.00	-3.50	80.00
												Fib[tp]	
20960820	2007.10.15 08:01	buy	2.00	gbpjpym	240.00	240.10	241.22	2007.10.15 13:38	240.54	0.00	0.00	0.00	91.63
								16384				FR022	
20959254	2007.10.15 07:15	buy	1.00	eurjpym	166.96	167.15	167.76	2007.10.15 13:39	167.58	0.00	0.00	0.00	52.60
								16384				FR0211015	
20959251	2007.10.15 07:15	buy	4.00	gbpjpym	239.60	239.70	241.22	2007.10.15 13:38	240.55	0.00	0.00	0.00	322.39
								16384				FR021	
20955576	2007.10.15 00:00	buy	1.00	eurjpym	166.70	165.91	167.50	2007.10.15 03:00	166.52	0.00	0.00	0.00	-15.31
								16384				FR0211014	
20953768	2007.10.12 19:00	buy	4.00	eurjpym	166.70	165.91	167.50	2007.10.12 19:30	166.62	0.00	0.00	0.00	-27.22
								16384				FR0211012	
20953122	2007.10.12 16:29	sell	1.00	eurusdm	1.4174	1.4276	1.4117	2007.10.16 07:50	1.4169	0.00	0.00	0.56	5.00
												Type1	

FIGURE 11.1   Interbank FX, LLC (*Cont.*)

20948275	2007.10.12 12:45	buy	2.00	gbpjpym	239.13	237.93	240.31	2007.10.12 16:13	239.07	0.00	0.00	0.00	-10.21
									16384			FR022	
20947093	2007.10.12 12:30	buy	4.00	gbpjpym	238.74	237.93	240.31	2007.10.12 14:00	238.92	0.00	0.00	0.00	61.28
									16384			FR021	
20945545	2007.10.12 10:59	buy	2.00	eurjpym	166.71	165.79	167.51	2007.10.12 15:00	166.39	0.00	0.00	0.00	-54.51
									16384			FR0211012	
20944609	2007.10.12 09:26	sell	2.00	gbpjpym	237.99	238.37	237.12	2007.10.12 12:09	238.37	0.00	0.00	0.00	-64.70
												Fib[sl]	
										0.00	0.00	29.40	5 110.78
												Closed P/L:	5 140.18

Open Trades:

Ticket	Open Time	Type	Size	Item	Price	S / L	T / P		Price	Commission	Taxes	Swap	Profit
						No transactions							
										0.00	0.00	0.00	0.00
												Floating P/L:	0.00

Working Orders:

Ticket	Open Time	Type	Size	Item	Price	S / L	T / P	Market Price		
21323279	2007.11.01 12:55	sell stop	8.00	eurusdm	1.4403	1.4459	1.4388	1.4409		Trend line Breakout

Summar y:

Deposit/Withdrawal:	0.00	Credit Facility:	0.00		
Closed Trade P/L:	5 140.18	Floating P/L:	0.00	Margin:	0.00
Balance:	7 288.37	Equity:	7 288.37	Free Margin:	7 288.37

Details:

Gross Profit:	7 888.22	Gross Loss:	2 748.04	Total Net Profi t:	5 140.18
Profit Factor:	2.87	Expected Payoff:	34.97		
Absolute Drawdown:	110.67	Maximal Drawdown:	1 038.47 (17.34%)	Relative Drawdown:	17.34% (1 038.47)

Total Trades:	147	Short Positions (won %):	61 (72.13%)	Long Positions (won %):	86 (86.05%)
		Profit Trades (% of total):	118 (80.27%)	Loss trades (% of total):	29 (19.73%)
Largest		profit trade:	358.90	loss trade:	-595.96
Average		profit trade:	66.85	loss trade:	-94.76
Maximum		consecutive wins ($):	14 (1 164.33)	consecutive losses ($):	4 (-107.25)
Maximal		consecutive profit (count):	1 164.33 (14)	consecutive loss (count):	-992.51 (3)
Average		consecutive wins:	7	consecutive losses:	2

FIGURE 11.1 Interbank FX, LLC (*Cont.*)

When trading I do not attempt to get 50 or 100 trades in a row without any losses like my colleague and friend Donald Snellgrove of Concorde Forex Group, Inc. But, I do attempt to get as much profit as possible and trade with higher-risk decisions than he does. I am probably not as good a trader, but that is not important. What is important is for you, as an aspiring trader, to benefit from our experience and counsel.

Ten Pips per Day

T he title of this appendix is provocative and certainly challenging, but it demonstrates the importance of using small profit targets when trading the Forex.

Table A.1 shows the growth of an account based upon a daily growth rate of 10 pips for one lot traded compounded. This might be unrealistic, but it underscores the importance of 10 pips daily. Some traders are interested in making massive profits, while at the same time smaller, but consistent profits are significant.

TABLE A.1 Growth of an Account Based on Daily Growth Rate of 10 Pips for One Lot Traded Compounded

Day	Total	Day	Total
Day 10	100	Day 20	110
Day 30	121	Day 40	133
Day 50	146	Day 60	161
Day 70	177	Day 80	195
Day 90	214	Day 100	236
Day 110	259	Day 120	285
Day 130	313	Day 140	345
Day 150	379	Day 160	417
Day 170	460	Day 180	505
Day 190	556	Day 200	612
Day 210	673	Day 220	740
Day 230	814	Day 240	895
Day 250	985		

About the Author

G erald "Gerry" Greene has worked primarily as a software engineer and consultant for most of his 40-year career. In 2001 he was introduced to Donald Snellgrove, who at that time was forming Concorde Forex Group, Inc. for the purpose of providing education services to Forex traders worldwide. As a senior vice president for CFG, he developed the proprietary charting software that is used by CFG traders. He has also been heavily involved in supporting all aspects of the CFG educational programs.

He posts his Forex market opinions on the Internet three times each day at www.cfgtrading.com for Concorde Forex Group traders worldwide. He can be reached via email at gegreene1@earthlink.net.

Index